50 THINGS THEY DON'T WANT YOU TO KNOW ABOUT TRUMP

ALSO BY JEROME HUDSON

50 Things They Don't Want You to Know

50 THINGS THEY DON'T WANT YOU TO KNOW ABOUT TRUMP

JEROME HUDSON

BROADSIDE BOOKS
An Imprint of HarperCollinsPublishers

HarperCollins books may be purchased for educational, business, or sales promotional use. For information, please email the Special Markets Department at SPsales@harpercollins.com.

Broadside Books™ and the Broadside logo are trademarks of HarperCollins Publishers.

FIRST EDITION

Library of Congress Cataloging-in-Publication Data

Names: Hudson, Jerome, author.
Title: 50 things they don't want you to know about Trump / Jerome Hudson.
Description: First edition. | [New York]: Broadside Books, [2020] |
    Summary: "National bestselling author and Breitbart.com editor Jerome
    Hudson returns with a list of the Trump administration's accomplishments
    the mainstream media has worked hardest to hide"— Provided by
    publisher.
Identifiers: LCCN 2020030729 | ISBN 9780063027657 (trade paperback) | ISBN
    9780063027664 (ebook)
Subjects: LCSH: Trump, Donald, 1946- | United States—Politics and
    government—2017- | Presidents—United States.
Classification: LCC E912 .H83 2020 | DDC 973.933092—dc23
LC record available at https://lccn.loc.gov/2020030729

ISBN 978-0-06-302765-7

20 21 22 23 24 LSC 10 9 8 7 6 5 4 3 2 1

To Wynton

CONTENTS

CONTENTS

50 THINGS THEY DON'T WANT YOU TO KNOW ABOUT TRUMP

PREFACE

Donald Trump loves to be front page news. If he loses reelection in November, the next four years will still be filled with arguments over whatever *former* President Trump tweets or says every day. Until he passes from this earth, the only thing people will want to talk about is whatever Donald Trump wants us to talk about. But that means we rarely discuss what he's actually *done*: the policies he's promoted, the facts about what's actually happened in the country on his watch.

50 Things They Don't Want You to Know About Trump is a collection of those facts. Snapshots of the past four years you're not likely to find anywhere else. And that's not by accident. The media narrative around Trump's first term is very different from what you're presented with on cable and network news, on NPR, or in your local paper. This book will help you cut through the fog of misinformation to see Donald Trump's record for what it really is.

Trump's White House run defied a century of political tradition. He toppled two political dynasties: Jeb Bush in the primary and Hillary Clinton in the general. Trump's candidacy was a threat to the corrupt political class of wealthy elites we pay to represent our interests. His election was a wholesale rejection of the callous culture that has corrupted Washington, D.C., and the globalist delusions that have enriched communist China at the expense of the free world.

The elite press didn't take Trump seriously. Nor did the pollsters, the pundits, his political rivals, the think tank honchos, Wall Street brass, Hollywood luminaries, or many of the leading academics— the very people in power, presiding over a political and economic system that wasn't benefiting a large share of the country in 2016.

Donald Trump didn't create the problems these elites had long ignored. Given the choice between Trump and Hillary Clinton—a corrupt, calculating relic of the system that created the mess—voters chose whom they saw to be a maverick. After surveying the china shop built by decades of bipartisan D.C. conventional wisdom, powerful business lobbyists, and globalist fantasies, Americans voted for the bull.

Among Trump's many enemies is a press corps consisting almost entirely of pious partisans devoted to ruinous reportage at the expense of honest journalism. The media charged with covering Donald Trump's presidency was publishing articles fantasizing about his impeachment nearly a year before he was sworn into office.

Of course, that's the kind of folly you'd expect from journalists, reporters, editors, and TV news anchors who donated to Trump's opponent by a margin of 96 percent to 4. It was still an Olympian display of arrogance from an American press corps whose record is clogged with incidents of laziness, incompetence, and political bias, from failing to foresee the War on Terror to missing the gathering storm of the housing collapse and 2008 financial crisis. From the early days of the Trump 2016 campaign to the closing months of Trump's first term, the media spent more time indulging conspiracy theories, weaving political narratives, and simply inventing stories than it did on reporting the facts.

The *Washington Post* suggested that Donald Trump could start a nuclear war and no one would be able to stop him. The media ran wild reporting a poll, backed by a group of Never-Trump Republicans, that said nearly half the country believed Trump would use a nuclear warhead against ISIS or a foreign enemy. Liberal economist Paul Krugman was among the many who predicted Trump's election would throw the world into a "permanent global recession." *The Guardian* columnist Jonathan Freedland said a Trump presidency would mean the end of civilization.

Of course, none of these things happened. And every one of those wild predictions was made before Trump had even won the election or been sworn into office!

The media's scorched earth treatment of Trump cost the country. The time they devoted to tearing down the administration was time they didn't spend reporting what the Trump White House was actually getting done.

The press constantly castigated Trump as racist. But they didn't tell you that he has allocated more funding to historically black colleges and universities than any other president in history. Or that Trump secured a massive donation worth billions in AIDS medication. Or that he placed $291 million in his 2020 Health and Human Services budget focused on ending the HIV epidemic by 2030. These moves would have a disproportionate impact on black Americans, who represent some 13 percent of the country's population but account for roughly 40 percent of new HIV infections. Did you know that black women–owned new businesses had the highest rate of growth of any group in the number of new firms between 2018 and 2019?

The media cranked out endless listicles declaring Trump a danger to the environment but downplayed the fact that the U.S. once again led the world in reducing carbon emissions in 2018 and 2019. Did you know that Trump authorized the largest wilderness preservation expansion in a decade?

Flint, Michigan's lead-laced water was a bludgeon used by the American left to beat conservatives over the head for half a decade. The Obama-led federal government couldn't seem to solve the problem. The truth is that Trump's Environmental Protection Agency finally fixed Flint's broken water infrastructure system.

There were thousands of news articles about Trump's January 2017 order temporarily barring most citizens from Iraq, Syria, Iran, Sudan, Libya, Somalia, and Yemen from entering the United States. What the media didn't tell you was that Trump's order listed the exact same seven countries that were named in a law signed by Barack Obama in December 2015. The media dubbed Trump's order a "Muslim ban" but they didn't want you to know that this so-called Muslim ban did not apply to 87 percent of the world's Muslim population.

The anti-Trump animus among many in the mainstream media had degenerated into full-blown anti-Trump psychosis by the halfway mark of his first term. This helped set the stage for the Democrats' campaign to impeach President Trump. The "genesis" for impeachment, Representative Al Green (D-TX) revealed in December 2019, "was when the president was running for office." The media went from breathlessly doubting Trump's chances of winning the presidential election to willing and eager participants in the Democrats' crusade to overturn it.

In early 2016, the Clinton campaign took over from Republican billionaire Paul Singer the funding of Fusion GPS's efforts to find anti-Trump dirt ahead of the election. Fusion GPS, the Washington, D.C.–based research firm, proceeded to hire ex-British spy Christopher Steele, who put together a "dossier" based on sketchy sources—including Russian sources—who claimed Trump and his campaign members colluded with Russia during the 2016 election. It also claimed that Trump had requested Russian prostitutes perform a "golden showers" show when he was in Moscow in 2013. Fusion GPS shopped the Democrat-funded, thinly sourced dossier around to journalists, members of Congress, and various government agencies.

By late July 2016, the dossier made its way to the FBI, which launched an investigation into the Trump campaign and key staffers. Beginning in fall 2016, the FBI used the dossier to obtain four consecutive secret surveillance warrants on former campaign aide Carter Page. After the election, top officials in the Obama administration decided to brief Trump on the dossier. That briefing leaked to CNN, prompting *BuzzFeed*, which had photographs of the dossier, to publish it in full. This sparked a congressional investigation into whether Trump had colluded with Russia.

House Intelligence Committee ranking member Adam Schiff (D-CA) then used the dossier as evidence that Trump had colluded with the Russians, even reading from it during a congressional hearing.

After Trump fired FBI Director James Comey in mid-2017, Comey leaked memos that paved the way for then-Acting Attorney General Rod Rosenstein to appoint a special counsel to investigate collusion between the Trump campaign and the Kremlin. Special Counsel Robert Mueller presided over a two-year-long, multimillion-dollar investigation into collusion. In March 2019, the Justice Department issued a summary of the Mueller investigation, revealing it found no evidence of a criminal conspiracy between the Trump campaign and Russia.

Still, Democrats in Congress—led by Schiff—argued Trump had colluded with Russia and obstructed justice and should be impeached. This came less than a year away from another presidential election. During his opening statement at the Senate impeachment trial, Schiff, the lead impeachment manager, let the mask slip, arguing that "the President's misconduct cannot be decided at the ballot box, for we cannot be assured that the vote will be fairly won."

House Speaker Nancy Pelosi (D-CA) initially opposed impeaching President Trump unless there was bipartisan support. She was echoing a strong statement made by Representative Jerry Nadler (D-NY), who in December 1998 said on the House floor: "There must never be an impeachment supported by one of our major political parties and opposed by the other." Nadler abandoned that thinking when he agreed to participate in the 100 percent partisan Democrat impeachment of Trump. In September 2019, Adam Schiff revealed a "whistleblower" complaint about a July 2019 phone call between Trump and Ukrainian president Volodymyr Zelensky, during which Trump urged Zelensky to look into Joe Biden and his son's alleged corruption in Ukraine. That complaint provided the political cover Pelosi needed to kick-start impeachment proceedings.

In April 2020, it came to light that President Obama had directed the FBI to continue investigating Trump's incoming national security adviser, Michael Flynn, and that Vice President Joe Biden had suggested justifying the investigation on the grounds that Flynn violated the obscure 1799 Logan Act, thereby keeping the collusion case alive.

That's how unelected bureaucrats, Democratic politicians, and a bevy of senior Obama officials used a dubious dossier funded by Hillary Clinton's campaign to kneecap Donald Trump's campaign, and eventually his presidency. And the American media were gleeful accomplices in this attempted coup.

On the December day that Democrats announced two articles of impeachment against Trump, the president's average job approval rating was higher than Obama's was on the same day during his first term in office, according to RealClearPolitics. At an average approval rating of 45 percent, President Trump's approval was roughly two percentage points above Obama's at the same time in his presidency. Trump was impeached a week later, and a month after that there was little evidence that voters cared. In fact, there was mounting evidence that on virtually every major indicator—the economy, national security, crime—Americans believed they were better off in 2020 than they were at the end of Obama's presidency. Americans satisfied with their personal life hit a four-decade high, according to Gallup polling released in February 2020. Two in three Americans also said they were *very* satisfied with life, another record high.

At the end of the day, what mattered most to Americans is that they were better off. The media didn't devote much coverage to it but it was Trump's economy that saw blue-collar workers enjoy three times the wage growth of the top 1 percent of households.

Even the *New York Times* had to admit that "Black Workers' Wages Are Finally Rising" in a February 2020 headline.

Much of this book is dedicated to China, the communist country that President Trump has crafted a multifaceted strategy to decouple from. The need for decoupling was never more blatantly obvious than when China became the epicenter of the novel coronavirus pandemic that plunged the world into economic calamity. The coronavirus changed everything and reset the 2020 presidential campaign by crippling President Trump's tremendous advantage on the economy and setting the stage for violence and hysteria after the police killing of George Floyd in Milwaukee—a city ruled with an iron fist by Democrats for generations. The Chinese virus didn't just reshuffle the deck for the 2020 election. It threw the game table in the air and sent cards flying.

One sector of the American economy squeezed hard by the coronavirus crisis was the media. China caused the crisis and then sat back while America's gullible elite press peddled propaganda and whitewashed the Chinese Communist Party lies that brought Black Plague-level death and economic misery to the entire world. Only too late did the American press realize their own industry would be among those ravaged by the economic fallout from the pandemic. They apparently assumed that since they could all work from home, and much of "journalism" these days involves scrolling through Twitter and Instagram feeds, they wouldn't suffer as much from the lockdowns as blue-collar workers. They were wrong again.

China has a starring role in America's deadly drug crisis, too, as the source for the deadly fentanyl that is littering our cities— and despairing rural communities—with corpses. The opioid crisis became a huge story under the Trump administration, including a good deal of misguided coverage that looked at decades-old data to blame prescription drug abuse instead of China's fentanyl and other deadly street drugs. We ended up with a war on prescription pain medication because big drug companies are a much easier target than street gangs whose cross-border connections could raise inconvenient questions about open-borders immigration policy.

If there is one constant theme linking the fifty facts presented in this book, it is the failure of the Beltway conventional wisdom that Trump ran against, the entirely rational loss of public faith in hyper-politicized "experts," and the bubbled media that amplifies their pronouncements. The corridors of power in Washington are bubbling with elegant theories and billion-dollar schemes that fall apart as soon as scrutiny is applied to those theories. This book is a steady dose of much-needed scrutiny.

Of *course* minority communities benefited tremendously from President Trump's growth policies, even as Democrats and their "experts" sneered it was all just a big tax-cut giveaway to the rich. Of *course* Trump tightening control on immigration pushed American wages up, despite a blizzard of impeccably credentialed white papers that assured us flooding the market with cheap imported labor—often paid under the table and thus avoiding the expensive overhead of legal employment—has no negative effect on wages at all. Of *course* it's possible to reduce the flood of illegal immigration by shutting down the benefits that draw people across the border and tightening enforcement.

Of *course* the end of net neutrality regulations helped the Internet instead of hurting it, despite a thousand doomsday prophecies flying from the social media accounts of Hollywood celebrities and Democrats, who claimed net neutrality repeal would *kill people*. Of *course* Trump is tougher on China, Russia, Iran, and other bad actors than Obama and Democrats ever were, or ever will be. Trump actually thinks America is right and good and has both the moral stature and economic power to press its case!

This is not a pro-Trump book. If you're as annoyed with *National Review* as you are with MSNBC, this book will confirm you've been told less than half the real story. Trump didn't get everything right. And the political and economic one-two punch of the coronavirus pandemic and left-wing riots was a combo few leaders could take without ending up on the ropes. But his track record of policy success compares very favorably with his recent predecessors.

50 Things They Don't Want You to Know About Trump will give you a chance to judge for yourself.

1.

DRUG OVERDOSES DROPPED FOR THE FIRST TIME IN THIRTY YEARS UNDER TRUMP

Nearly 64,000 Americans died from a drug overdose in 2016 alone. Opioid overdoses accounted for more than 42,000 of these deaths, more than any previous year on record. The number of overdose deaths increased for the next two years. Then, 2018 marked the end of a grim chapter in American history—or, pessimists say, perhaps a blip interrupting an otherwise irreversible trend. Either way, it was historic.

By mid-2019, the U.S. Centers for Disease Control (CDC) had preliminary data from 2018 showing that, for the first time since 1990, the number of drug overdose deaths in America dropped. In July 2019 the *New York Times* cited the CDC, reporting that 68,557 people died of drug overdoses in 2018, representing a 5 percent drop from 2017, which saw about 72,000 deaths. By January 2020, the CDC revealed that the final, verified number of overdose deaths in 2018 was even lower: 67,367, a 6.4 percent drop.

"The decline was due almost entirely to a dip in deaths from prescription opioid painkillers, the medicines that set off the epidemic of addiction that has lasted nearly two decades," the *New York Times* noted in its July report. The final statistics said the same.

The dramatic change in overdose rates fueled a modest increase in overall American life expectancy, something that had failed to happen in 2015, at the height of the drug crisis.

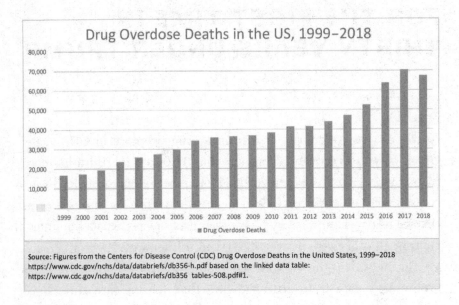

Drug Overdose Deaths in the US, 1999–2018

Source: Figures from the Centers for Disease Control (CDC) Drug Overdose Deaths in the United States, 1999–2018
https://www.cdc.gov/nchs/data/databriefs/db356-h.pdf based on the linked data table:
https://www.cdc.gov/nchs/data/databriefs/db356 tables-508.pdf#1.

Even the bad news from the CDC's report was, for once, slightly less bad. While deaths due to heroin and prescription painkillers declined, the number of deaths attributable to fentanyl increased that year. But they increased at a slightly less dramatic rate than they had in the immediate past, suggesting a full reversal on the horizon. Fentanyl is an opioid painkiller up to 100 times more potent than morphine that, thanks largely to the Chinese government, has flooded the American drug market. Opioid addicts make up most of the fentanyl overdose deaths. Faced with stricter doctors who no longer refill prescriptions for painkillers, opioid addicts may seek an alternative on the street. Consuming fentanyl in amounts similar to less-concentrated opioids, like prescription painkillers, makes overdose incredibly likely. "Between 2013 and 2016, it [the fentanyl overdose rate] was doubling pretty much every year. If it's less than doubling, I guess you can call that an improvement," Dr. Holly Hedegaard, an injury epidemiologist at the CDC's National Center for Health Statistics, told *U.S. News & World Report* in January 2020.

The CDC's numbers still reflected a national tragedy but, for the first time since the opioid crisis gripped American communities, it felt like it might one day end. This positive shift followed the Trump White House's concerted effort to change the medical culture around opioids, keep deadly drugs off the market, and provide victims of the crisis access to lifesaving treatments. In 2017, his first year in office, President Donald Trump declared the opioid crisis a national emergency and mobilized diverse sectors of his administration to combat the scourge in a holistic manner. Trump's team reframed what had previously been considered almost exclusively a healthcare matter, recognizing it as a crisis that extended beyond public health into border control, illegal immigration, and foreign policy. Rather than concentrating only on access to drugs that prevent overdoses, the Trump administration targeted the sources of deadly, illegal forms of opioids to take them off the market, while also pressuring the pharmaceutical companies and doctors to stop overprescribing legal opioids. He and First Lady Melania Trump also gave the issue prominence in a way that not only conveyed the urgency of the problem, but also treated addicts with respect—considering them victims, not criminals.

Certainly, Trump can't declare victory on this one quite yet, but to understand why is to know exactly how severely opioids had corrupted American medical culture. Trump couldn't launch a Reagan-style "just say no" campaign against opioids because, unlike the cocaine and ketamine of the 1980s, opioids were being prescribed by doctors. Opioid crisis victims are not just lost souls seeking a physical escape from their dreary lives—they are, often, people dealing with illness whose only sin was to trust a doctor. They did everything right: They promptly visited a medical professional when they felt physically unwell, and they took the remedies the expert recommended. But they still wound up addicted to drugs. Those with chronic pain from injuries, arthritis, or other conditions also received opioid prescriptions liberally for much of the 2010s. Individuals undergoing nearly every possible type of surgery were also among those preyed on by doctors in that decade, according to a study by the Johns Hopkins School of Public Health and Kaiser Health News.

Doctors didn't need more excuses to prescribe opioids, or more patients to corrupt, but the Affordable Care Act (ACA) helped with that anyway. Signed in 2010 but officially activated in 2014, the ACA's Medicaid expansion, liberals will note, greatly expanded access to drugs like naloxone, used to save someone overdosing and reverse the effects of opioids. Unfortunately, it also greatly increased access to opioids. "For dangerous opioids such as oxycodone, Medicaid co-pays can run as low as $1 for as many as 240 pills—pills that can be sold for up to $4,000 on the street," a 2018 report by the Senate's Committee on Security and Governmental Affairs observed. This incentivized people with opioid prescriptions to sell at high prices, fueling addicts but also giving them reason to continue asking for refills, even if they had been prescribed far more opioids than necessary after surgery.

The Senate report found that the black market for opioids grew much more organized and lucrative as the ACA (also known as

Obamacare) began to take form, creating rings of drug sales that targeted people in need:

> **In one Connecticut case, a ringleader recruited Medicaid beneficiaries to obtain nearly $200,000 of oxycodone from pharmacies through forged prescriptions. "He preyed on a lot of low-income people with Medicaid cards," according to a police lieutenant who helped oversee the investigation. Pharmacists "were very trusting just because it was Medicaid," said the lieutenant, who added: "Absolutely, Medicaid is what allowed him to make so much money."**

While financially beneficial to drug companies and doctors, Obamacare's opioid near-giveaways did nothing to help insurance companies, which were stuck footing the bill for patients not on Medicare under the ACA's protocol. Insurers ultimately began crafting coverage plans with limited aid for drugs like naloxone, or opioids themselves, in what RealClearHealth called a "race to the bottom." Insurance companies' aim was to shoo away patients whom, under Obamacare, they would have been forced to cover.

This started to happen just as the CDC had begun to implement new guidelines for prescribing opioids in an attempt to limit access to these dangerous drugs, which had previously been more widely available. Thus, an increase in heroin and fentanyl overdose deaths, a decrease in prescription opioid deaths, and the ongoing implementation of Obamacare provisions all began in 2015.

The CDC identified a 72.2 percent increase in deaths due to fentanyl and other synthetic opioids between 2014 and 2015. Over that same period, deaths from heroin increased 20.6 percent, but deaths from natural or semi-synthetic opioids increased only 2.6 percent, an order of magnitude less than deaths from heroin. Meanwhile, deaths from methadone decreased.

Sixty-four thousand people died of opioid overdoses in 2016, the year before Trump took office. In 2017, he declared the crisis a public health emergency and has since donated his presidential salary on multiple occasions to organizations involved in the fight against opioids. He has also turned his attention to cutting off addiction at its source by stemming unnecessary and imprudent opioid prescriptions, keeping deadly synthetic opioids off the streets, expanding access to live-saving drugs, and cutting the flow of illegally trafficked heroin into the country.

Trump proposed a plan to curb prescriptions and trafficking in 2018, including a "Safer Prescribing Plan" intended to cut opioid prescriptions by a third that year. He did not limit himself to awareness campaigns, as he increased legal penalties for those who traffic in fentanyl (and, somewhat infamously, proposed capital punishment for drug traffickers in extreme cases). His holistic approach also involved the use of the FDA to shut down websites that sold opioids with no oversight, often from abroad, and to inspect mail flows for the illegal shipment of opioids.

Then came the sanctions and drug busts to limit the deadliest opioids' access to the American public. The U.S. Treasury heavily sanctioned known Chinese fentanyl traffickers. Law enforcement agents reported hauling in astronomical amounts of Chinese fentanyl meant for the U.S. black market. One drug bust, in August 2019, yielded enough fentanyl to kill 14 million people.

Shutting down the flow of Chinese fentanyl into the United

States required at least some acknowledgment from China that their country was part of the problem. When Trump first declared opioid addiction a national emergency, China was too busy issuing bigoted statements about American culture to have time to help. "As many states decriminalize marijuana, the public's attitudes and trends of thinking toward drugs will also have a bad effect," Yu Haibin of the China National Narcotics Control Commission, the top drug official in the communist regime, said in December 2017, blaming a "lax cultural attitude" for the opioid crisis. "The United States should look within to cut down demand for opioids which are fueling its deadly drug crisis rather than stressing unsubstantiated claims that China is the major source of these chemicals."

After two years of an emboldened policy toward China—one that elevated the concerns of allies like Taiwan, condemned China's human rights atrocities on the world stage, and forced China into difficult trade negotiations—Beijing finally admitted that its fentanyl production was as prodigious as suggested and agreed to help the Trump administration limit its distribution. The Communist Party has never met a promise it isn't willing to break, so the agreement is far from a victory, but for a country as obsessed with reputation as China, the admission and agreement was a significant step forward.

Policies on the southern border also helped limit the influx of heroin and fentanyl into the United States. President Trump campaigned largely on a promise to secure the border from the menace of wealthy violent Mexican drug cartels operating on the other side. The wall may not yet be built, but millions of dollars' worth of fentanyl and heroin, including the arrest of one individual caught with enough fentanyl to kill 500,000 people, will no longer make it to the American black market.

2.

PRESIDENT TRUMP HAS ALLOCATED MORE FUNDING TO HISTORICALLY BLACK COLLEGES AND UNIVERSITIES THAN ANY OTHER PRESIDENT

In May 2017, President Trump promised "unwavering support" for the nation's historically black colleges and universities (HBCUs). By the time he had made that declaration, the president had already signed an executive order establishing the White House Initiative to Promote Excellence and Innovation at Historically Black Colleges and Universities. The order made HBCUs part of a White House federal initiative, shifting responsibility from the Department of Education. It also established the President's Board of Advisors on HBCUs. "With this executive order, we will make HBCUs a priority in the White House—an absolute priority," Trump said during a February 2017 signing ceremony. "A lot of people are going to be angry that they're not a priority, but that's OK," Trump told the presidents of nearly 100 HBCUs gathered in the Oval Office.

The measure was merely the first of many moves President Trump would make to prioritize funding for America's 102 HBCUs.

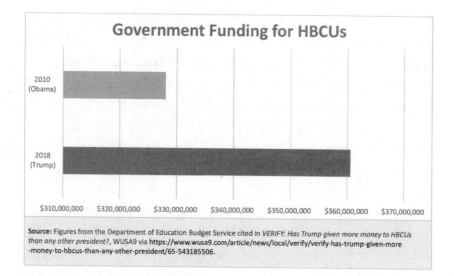

Government Funding for HBCUs

Source: Figures from the Department of Education Budget Service cited in *VERIFY: Has Trump given more money to HBCUs than any other president?*, WUSA9 via https://www.wusa9.com/article/news/local/verify/verify-has-trump-given-more-money-to-hbcus-than-any-other-president/65-543185506.

"In March 2018, the Trump administration provided financial relief to HBCUs impacted by Hurricanes Katrina and Rita that struck the Gulf Coast in 2005," *Black Enterprise* reported. "Secretary of Education Betsy DeVos issued full forgiveness of loans in the amount of $322 million to Dillard University, Southern University at New Orleans, Tougaloo College, and Xavier University of Louisiana under the HBCU Hurricane Supplemental Loan program. The monies saved can be repurposed to provide tuition assistance and expansion of curriculum, where feasible." The rule kicked off instant condemnation from consumer advocates.

"She was genuinely interested in working on our behalf," said Walter Kimbrough, president of Dillard University in New Orleans, which received loan relief thanks to DeVos's decision. "That's their big win," he said of the administration's work with HBCUs. President

Trump continued to support a historically black college and university system that had been weakened in recent years. College closures, declining enrollment, and scant finances contributed to the rising risk of these schools losing their accreditation. Trump vowed to break the logjam in Congress over the funding for HBCUs. By the end of 2018, he had appropriated more than $360 million to HBCUs. The massive figure put him in the record books as having allocated more money to HBCUs than any other president in history.

In December 2019, President Trump signed a bipartisan bill, known as the FUTURE Act. The law permanently reauthorized hundreds of millions of dollars in federal funding to historically black colleges and universities. The Trump-signed bill also simplified the process of the Free Application for Federal Student Aid (FAFSA) by eliminating more than twenty questions from the application form and simplifying the repayment process for roughly eight million borrowers. "When I took office, I promised to fight for HBCUs, and my administration continues to deliver," Trump said at the time. "A few months ago, funding for HBCUs was in jeopardy. But the White House and Congress came together and reached a historic agreement."

Michael Lomax, the president and CEO of the United Negro College Fund (UNCF), praised the president and the thousands of advocates responsible for getting the legislation becoming law. "We enlisted more than 20,000 supporters to write and call their members of Congress. This activated army of advocates became the front line of support for HBCUs, and they won the battle for our institutions," Lomax said.

UNCF senior vice president for public policy and government affairs Lodriguez Murray also showered President Trump with praise. "The last time a law like this passed and was signed in this manner was nineteen years ago this month," said Murray. "Stand-alone bills like the FUTURE Act that focus solely on minority populations and have a substantial benefit to HBCUs rarely pass Congress like this. They usually become part of larger, must-pass pieces of legislation; however, the FUTURE Act stood on its own two feet. The Minority Health and Health Disparities Research and Education Act of 2000, Public Law 106–525, was the last bill to become law like the FUTURE Act. This is a once-a-generation oc-currence, and UNCF couldn't be prouder to make a difference for HBCUs and our students."

The bill would restore roughly $255 million in annual funding, which was much needed after Congress had failed to renew fund-ing for HBCUs. When black colleges and universities were facing a lapse in federal funding, some schools had planned deep cuts, which included the elimination of many faculty positions and school programs. Senator Lamar Alexander (R-TN), the chairman of the Health, Education, Labor, and Pensions (HELP) Committee, called the bill a "Christmas present for college students and their families." Alexander noted that the bill would also eliminate unnecessary and burdensome red tape regarding the FAFSA. "This bipartisan pro-vision stops families from having to give their same tax informa-tion to the federal government twice—first to the IRS, then again to the U.S. Department of Education," Alexander added. "It should eliminate most of the so-called 'verification' process, which is a bu-reaucratic nightmare that 5.5 million students go through annually."

Secretary DeVos called the FUTURE Act a "historic bill" that reflects the administration's commitment to students.

President Trump's securing of permanent funding for HBCUs was not solely recognized by Republicans and Trump administration officials. The mainstream media also took notice. *USA Today* noted in September 2019 that "under the Trump administration, federal funding for HBCUs has increased by more than $100 million over the last two years, a 17 percent increase since 2017." That month, President Trump spoke to the National Historically Black Colleges and Universities Week Conference, in which he touted his work to improve HBCUs. He said:

> **Over the past two and a half years, we have listened and learned from you, and we have taken very, very major action. I think you know that. I signed legislation to increase federal funding for HBCUs by a record 13 percent. That was the highest ever done . . .**
>
> **Today, I'm thrilled to announce another major action we're taking to protect HBCUs. Previously, federal law restricted more than forty faith-based HBCUs and seminaries from fully accessing federal support for capital improvement projects. This meant that your faith-based institutions, which have made such extraordinary contributions to America, were unfairly punished for their religious beliefs. Did we know that? Did everybody know that? Because it was . . . that was not good.**

"This week, our Department of Justice has published an opinion declaring such discriminatory restrictions as unconstitutional,"

President Trump said. "It was a big step. And from now on, faith-based HBCUs will enjoy equal access to federal support."

The historic level of funding for America's historically black colleges and universities under Trump wouldn't stop there. Trump signed the CARES Act into law to help the millions of Americans whose lives were upended by the economic devastation caused by the spread of COVID-19 in March 2020. The law allocated $6.28 billion in financial relief from the U.S. Department of Education in the form of direct cash payments. More than $14 billion was set aside for the Higher Education Emergency Relief Fund. Of that, nearly 100 HBCUs received assistance of over $380 million. The money was intended to be dispersed as cash grants to university students affected by the deadly virus for food, housing, and healthcare.

3.

PRESCRIPTION DRUG PRICES FELL FOR THE FIRST TIME IN FIFTY YEARS DURING TRUMP'S TENURE

Democrats and establishment media pundits (but I repeat myself) have spent years admonishing President Trump over his attempts to scale back or scrap Obamacare. These same politicians and pundits have also portrayed the president as maniacal and completely unsympathetic to the average American's healthcare plight. However, despite the establishment's narrative of the president's healthcare legacy, Trump has managed to lower the Affordable Care Act exchange premiums for the first time in the program's history. Trump has also managed to lower prescription drug prices for the first time since 1972.

For decades, presidents have promised to lower prescription drug prices, but they've all failed. Meanwhile, prescription drug prices continued to climb, outpacing general inflation for roughly fifty years. The White House Council of Economic Advisers (CEA) noted that prescription drug prices had continued to increase under President Obama. The CEA released a report in February 2020 that found that the president's actions managed to lower drug prices.

It found that, under President Trump, prescription drug prices are 12.7 percent lower than projected. According to the CEA, over the past two years, as of May 2019, prescription drug prices *decreased* by more than 11 percent, well below general inflation. "In 2018, prescription drug prices even declined in nominal terms over the calendar year for the first time since 1972," the CEA report said. "This past year, prescription drug prices experienced the largest year-over-year decline in more than fifty years."

The economic advisory council credited the decrease in prescription drug prices to the president's efforts to approve more generic and name-brand drugs at the Food and Drug Administration (FDA), and enhancing choice and price competition in the pharmaceutical markets. Under Trump, the FDA has approved a record number of generic and brand-name drugs. In at least one case, the CEA noted that the stock price of one foreign generic drug producer plummeted in July 2017, which analysts attributed to "greater competition as a result of an increase in generic approvals by the FDA."

The CEA estimated that Trump's prescription drug–targeted policies will reduce and save consumers roughly 10 percent on pharmaceuticals, which will result "in an increase of $32 billion per year in the purchasing power of the incomes of Americans (including consumers and producers)." The savings are due in large part, the CEA noted, to the 2017 Drug Competition Action Plan and the 2018 Strategic Policy Roadmap.

The CEA suggested that the president's actions on prescription drugs particularly helped lower-income households. The council stated the obvious, that costly regulations often impact lower-income Americans more than their wealthier counterparts. They wrote that "the poorest fifth of households spend 2.7 percent of their incomes out-of-pocket on prescription drugs, while the richest fifth of households spend only 0.3 percent." Along with the president's deregulatory actions in the Internet sector and prescription drugs, the report said, these two actions "represent 2.4 percent of the income for the poorest fifth of households, compared with 0.3 percent for the rich."

The data defies the familiar establishment logic that deregulation benefits only the rich and corporations and couldn't possibly be a boon to America's working class. "Deregulation is code for 'let the rich guys do whatever they want,'" Senator Elizabeth Warren (D-MA) said in the keynote speech of an event at Georgetown University Law School in June 2018. "The Trump administration and an army of lobbyists are determined to rig the game in their favor, to boost their own profit, the cost to the consumer be damned."

President Trump used his fourth State of the Union address to urge Congress to pass Senator Chuck Grassley's (R-IA) Prescription Drug Pricing Reduction Act. In an applause-filled prime-time speech, the president boasted about confronting Big Pharma: "We have approved a record number of affordable generic drugs, and medicines are being approved by the F.D.A. at a faster clip than ever before," Trump said. The president took a victory lap, celebrating the history achieved in 2019, when "for the first time in fifty-one years, the cost of prescription drugs actually went down."

> Working together, Congress can reduce drug prices substantially from current levels. I've been speaking to Senator Chuck Grassley of Iowa and others in

> Congress in order to get something on drug pricing done, and done quickly and properly. I'm calling for bipartisan legislation that achieves the goal of dramatically lowering prescription drug prices. Get a bill on my desk, and I will sign it into law immediately.
>
> —President Trump in his fourth
> State of the Union address

This chest thumping wasn't by accident. Just a few weeks after President Trump addressed the nation, the Kaiser Family Foundation released polling that showed healthcare ranked as the most important issue for all voters.

4.

AMERICA ONCE AGAIN LED THE WORLD IN REDUCING CARBON EMISSIONS IN 2019

I can actually feel some of you wincing at the title of this chapter. The truth is, whole swaths of the American electorate reject the doomsday warnings and climate hysteria from Democratic politicians and insufferable celebrity elites, and the endless lectures from Greta Thunberg about how we need to live in pods and eat bugs to save the planet from an environmental catastrophe. Lost in all the alarmism is the good news: Trump's America continues to lead the world in reducing its carbon footprint. Our success in cutting carbon output continues a trend that should be celebrated no matter your political persuasion. And we've done it without destroying our economy or enacting some twelve-figure government overhaul like the Green New Deal.

Consider the data. The International Energy Agency (IEA) is an intergovernmental organization designed to track the world's energy industries. They've become a leading source on data about carbon emissions worldwide. The IEA is by far more credible an outfit than, say, the Intergovernmental Panel on Climate Change (IPCC). (You may recall the IPCC as the group that widely publicized Michael Mann's discredited "hockey-stick" chart, which was erroneously heralded as evidence of catastrophic man-made climate change.) To be clear, the IEA is by no means a pro-Trump group. They're based in Paris, France, which no one would seriously consider MAGA Country.

The IEA's 2019 Report on Carbon Emissions

The United States saw the largest decline in energy-related CO_2 emissions in 2019 on a country basis—a fall of 140 Mt, or 2.9 percent, to 4.8 Gt. US emissions are now down almost 1 Gt from their peak in the year 2000, the largest absolute decline by any country over that period. A 15 percent reduction in the use of coal for power generation underpinned the decline in overall US emissions in 2019. Coal-fired power plants faced even stronger competition from natural gas-fired generation, with benchmark gas prices an average of 45 percent lower than 2018 levels. As a result, gas increased its share in electricity generation to a record high of 37 percent.

The largest decline on a country basis? Go team America!

If you're still dubious about why this drop deserves celebrating, you're not alone. After all, climate change doesn't matter to most U.S. voters. It doesn't even matter to the typical leftist! You think

I'm kidding? For years, Pew Research has been asking voters to rank 18 different issues by level of importance. "Dealing with global warming" ended up in second-to-last place in 2007, Climate Depot noted. From 2008 to 2013, it ranked last. Between 2017 and 2019 it ranked second to last. Junk or legitimate science aside, you should care about America lowering its carbon emissions. Not because it will save the planet. Most of us know that Queen Greta and her ilk shouldn't be lecturing America. They should be picketing in India and bombarding Beijing with their sanctimonious sermons. Air-quality watchdog AirVisual announced that twenty-one of the thirty worst polluted cities on Earth are in India. China would likely represent a much larger share of that list but that regime likely lied about their annual emissions data like they lie about everything else.

But it's a mistake to assume that lowering carbon emissions is just an environmental issue. It's also about modernization and greater economic efficiency. Calculating the U.S. decline in carbon emissions wasn't based on an economic downturn. Our country pared its emissions just as the overall economy grew. Put another way, Americans used more electricity and engaged in increased economic activity and we still led the world in reducing emissions. Second, 2019's reduction is part of a positive multiyear trend, so it's not a fluke. EPA data, which I included in *50 Things They Don't Want You to Know*, shows that as of 2018, "Carbon emissions from energy use from the U.S. are the lowest since 1992." Third, our carbon reductions are being realized as neither a government-backed carbon tax nor punishing regulations that rip apart America's energy economy, including the coal industry. In fact, the Trump EPA has helped shift the energy sector toward the modernization of equipment. When economic output is high and the economy is expanding, it makes sense to upgrade equipment. Modernizing equipment in the energy-production sector means greater energy efficiency and an overall reduction in carbon pollution. For example, "Modern electricity delivery technologies may increase the energy efficiency of the overall electricity system by reducing energy losses along transmission and distribution lines and delivering higher quality electricity to industry, businesses, and homes," the EPA notes. "Electricity usage data from smart meters may be used to support other energy efficiency efforts and reduce consumption." This all has the added advantage of amplifying our long-term environmental benefits.

If you want to see the hazards of a bureaucracy-mandated scheme to lower emissions, look no further than Canada. Prime Minister Justin Trudeau has endorsed a law forcing provinces to tax carbon emissions. As you can imagine, companies took their business elsewhere whenever possible, including to the United States. Ethan Allen Institute policy analyst David Flemming documented this trend, writing: "Foreign direct investment in Canada *fell 56 percent* from 2013 to 2017, which has caused Canada's prospects for economic growth to decrease. As a result, Trudeau has been forced to decrease his demands out of fear that his party would lose in the 2019 election." Spoiler alert! Canada hasn't come close to hitting its carbon emission targets.

Fourth, to celebrate our carbon reduction is to recognize the boom of natural gas in America. Trump's strategy of "energy dominance" has caused an explosion in natural gas output, including fracking. The shale revolution supported by fracking has been a huge driver of economic growth for states that allow it. Some states have banned fracking, namely New York, and have sat on the sidelines, missing out on a true economic revival. *Investor's Business Daily* observed:

Low energy prices, courtesy of the shale boom, have boosted discretionary income by $2,500 per year for a family of four, White House economists estimate. . . . The creation of hundreds of thousands of high-paying jobs, which helped spur recovery from the financial crisis, and low-cost energy for U.S. manufacturers are other big dividends from more than $1 trillion in cumulative investment, mostly across seven major shale regions.

The once-massive U.S. petroleum deficit—$436 billion in 2008—turned into a surplus last September.

Indeed, as I will cover in detail in chapter 24, America became a net exporter of natural gas in 2017.

According to the White House Council of Economic Advisers (CEA), "The Trump Administration's deregulatory policies aim to support private sector innovation and initiative by reducing excessively prescriptive government regulation. In doing so, the Administration seeks to further unleash the country's abundant human and energy resources." This is exactly what the IEA report shows. As you'll note in the snippet I included earlier, natural gas power plants now generate 37 percent of the electricity in America because fuel prices dropped 45 percent in just one year. Why did fuel prices drop? Because President Trump put America to work and removed as much of the swamp's red tape as possible. "We are independent, and we do not need Middle East oil," the president said, taking a victory lap in January 2020.

5.

TRUMP'S EPA GAVE $100 MILLION TO FIX THE BROKEN WATER INFRASTRUCTURE SYSTEM IN FLINT, MICHIGAN

The sad saga of lead-laced water in Flint, Michigan, became one of the American left's favorite talking points for half a decade. Flint residents were plagued by lead-spiked tap water for years. The Great Lakes State's lawmakers proved impotent and the full weight of the federal government couldn't seem to solve the problem—that is, until Donald Trump took over the White House. Many may ask, how did Flint become the left's poster child for what they view as American racism and persecution of poor people? (That's not an exaggeration.)

"It is hard to imagine this happening in a city that didn't have Flint's demographic profile—mostly black and disproportionately poor," Charles Blow wrote in the *New York Times*. Everyone's favorite failed presidential candidate, Hillary Clinton, said much the same in 2016.

> We've had a city in the United States of America where the population, which is poor in many ways

and majority African-American, has been drinking and bathing in lead-contaminated water. And
the governor of that state acted as though he didn't
really care. He had a request for help that he had basically stonewalled. I'll tell you what—if the kids in
a rich suburb of Detroit had been drinking contaminated water and being bathed in it, there would've
been action.

> —Hillary Clinton, blaming the Flint, Michigan,
> water crisis on the Republican governor

Throughout the Flint water crisis, which began in 2014, blame
was placed on the head of Republican governor Rick Snyder. If you
asked anyone from the mayor of Flint to then-presidential candidate
Clinton, it was Snyder's fault that Flint's water was tainted with
lead. Of course, there are two reasons Snyder was blamed: First, he
was the only Republican elected official around and, second, Donald
Trump wasn't president yet.

In fact, Flint, from top to bottom, had been a thoroughly
Democrat-run city. As explained by John Hayward of Breitbart
News:

**No, it's a Democrat issue. Democrats made this disaster
happen—Democrat city council, Democrat mayor, Democrat emergency manager (appointed to get along with the
Democrat local officials he was overseeing), Democrat**

state bureaucrats, and Democrat EPA. They made their horrendous decision to save money because decades of Democrat rule left Flint in a state of severe financial crisis—much worse than it needed to be, when the auto industry jobs in Flint went away. No citizen of Flint, from any racial background, has been disenfranchised—they voted for the people who did this to them.

Most people don't know what caused the Flint water crisis. The mainstream media and Democratic politicians would prefer you never know. Flint's citizens and businesses had been sucked dry by decades of foolish financial choices by their elected officials, who supplied substandard municipal services. But before April 2014, the water wasn't poisoned by lead. That all changed when Flint's Democratic leadership decided to end its decades-long water service from Detroit and instead pull its water supply from the Flint River. Flint's Democratic mayor at the time, Dayne Walling, bragged, "The water quality speaks for itself." But the Flint River's water lacked one critical component, the special treatment necessary to handle Flint's old lead pipes. The water was a dirty, lead-laced, undrinkable mess by the time it came out of Flint residents' showerheads and faucets.

As Hayward described, none of the Democrats in charge lifted a finger to fix Flint's water. The only government official in Michigan to take any responsibility was Governor Snyder. In January 2016, Snyder said in his State of the State speech, "To you, the people of Flint, I say tonight as I have before: I am sorry and I will fix it. Government failed you." But an honest reading of the timeline absolves Snyder of guilt. According to the governor's testimony before

Congress, the Michigan Department of Environmental Quality knew about Flint's problems nearly 18 months before it told him the full extent of the crisis in Flint.

It wasn't just Michigan officials who dropped the ball. Obama's Environmental Protection Agency (EPA) deserves plenty of blame. In the case of the federal response, or lack thereof, which was routinely theorized as racism, it's important to remember that it was a White House–led EPA *reporting to a black, Democratic president* that took no action.

The EPA inspector general's interim report on the Flint water crisis explains that the agency delayed its response by nearly seven months after Michigan pleaded for help. According to the report, a sensible EPA would have demonstrated "a greater sense of urgency" to "intervene when the safety of drinking water is compromised." Gee, ya think?

Like so many chapters in this book illustrate, the tide changed when Donald Trump assumed office. Suddenly, Flint's misery was no longer a foregone conclusion but instead another challenge for Trump to tackle. Despite the Democrats' never-ending propaganda that the man is racist, Trump has gone to bat time and time again for black Americans, with those in Flint, Michigan, being no exception. Trump launched his mission to fix Flint's water by cutting through the left's misinformation machine with a searing line that demonstrates the diminution decades of Democratic rule can create. "It used to be the cars made in Flint, and you couldn't drink the water in Mexico. Now the cars are made in Mexico, and you can't drink the water in Flint. But we're going to turn it all around," Trump said in November 2016 during a rally in Michigan.

By early 2017, it was clear to the Trump administration that the local and state levels of government would never be able to clean up Flint's water. It would take flexing federal muscles to fix Flint, which Trump's EPA brought to bear in the form of a $100 million grant to fund a project to replace Flint's bad pipes. The grant came with strict stipulations about the timelines for the project because, let's be honest, can you really trust a bunch of Democrats with $100 million?

There were various bumps in the road, like in any big government project. The city hired an incompetent contractor with little experience. But by the spring of 2019, Flint's water system was mostly fixed. You can go on social media today and find people complaining about dirty water in Flint, but even Trump-bashing NPR conceded in April 2019, "Tests have shown Flint's tap water has improved greatly since the depths of the water crisis. Now, it's well within federal and state standards for lead, even better than many other cities." And all it took was action by the president whom the left loves to call a racist and a hater of the poor, Donald Trump, to restore drinkable water to the residents of Flint—black and white, rich and poor.

6.

TRUMP APPOINTED AMERICA'S FIRST OPENLY GAY CABINET MEMBER

"Dangerous."

"Disastrous."

"Scary."

A "goon."

It would have been reasonable for the first openly gay cabinet member in U.S. history to expect some bigoted pushback on his ascent. After all, societal thinking on the acceptance of LGBT people in America has advanced at light speed in the past decade, as previous opposition to same-sex marriage from prominent progressives such as President Barack Obama and non-president Hillary Clinton prove. But for anyone but Richard Grenell, who briefly served as acting director of national intelligence, appointed by President Trump, that vitriol would have likely not come from far-left Hollywood and the mainstream media.

In February 2020, Trump became the first president to promote an openly LGBT person to such a high position, applauding Grenell for having been "highly respected" in his previous job, ambassador to Germany, the most prominent LGBT ambassador in U.S. history.

Donald J. Trump ✓
@realDonaldTrump

As we celebrate LGBT Pride Month and recognize the outstanding contributions LGBT people have made to our great Nation, let us also stand in solidarity with the many LGBT people who live in dozens of countries worldwide that punish, imprison, or even execute individuals....

3:12 PM · May 31, 2019 · Twitter for iPhone

Donald J. Trump ✓
@realDonaldTrump

....on the basis of their sexual orientation. My Administration has launched a global campaign to decriminalize homosexuality and invite all nations to join us in this effort!

3:12 PM · May 31, 2019 · Twitter for iPhone

"Rick has represented our Country exceedingly well and I look forward to working with him," Trump said, beaming. It is Grenell's responsibility to facilitate communication among the various federal government intelligence apparatuses, a job created after all these agencies failed to share information with one another that could have prevented the September 11, 2001, terrorist attacks. It is in his hands to ensure that when a critical piece of national security intelligence comes into any American agency, it is communicated to the people best equipped to use it.

Giving such a profoundly significant job to an LGBT person was Trump's way of sending two signals to the power brokers in American politics. First, to all observers, this showed that his was an accepting administration that did not see LGBT people as tokens given insignificant jobs for appearance's sake. The second was a more direct message to the establishment Republican Party: Business as usual under previous party leaders—the kind who allowed casual, unchallenged discrimination against LGBT people—was over, for good. Not that the Republican Party had not welcomed Grenell in the past. His prodigious resume got him into Trump's orbit to begin with, and was in part the product of being given opportunities to work within the GOP. Grenell held the post of spokesman for the U.S. Ambassador to the United Nations longer than anyone in history, from 2001 to 2008. He had been appointed by President George W. Bush and allowed to list his same-sex partner as an official plus-one to White House events. He had reached that post after working with moderate Republicans like Governor George Pataki of New York.

This acceptance was very limited. Grenell's tenure was marked by a yearslong battle with the State Department to treat his partner as a proper spouse. It was a battle he lost (protocol for State Department handling of same-sex partners changed under the Obama administration). Republicans lost the White House in 2008, on the eve of the populist eruption against them by what came to be known as the Tea Party. At that time, the GOP establishment loudly attempted to use bigotry against LGBT people to stake their claim to the entirety of American conservatism.

In 2010, the American Conservative Union (ACU) allowed GOProud, a newly minted conservative gay group, to participate in its annual conference, CPAC. This triggered a backlash from other socially conservative groups, some of whom spoke out at a conference that was supposed to be about individual freedom and small government to disagree with fellow participants' sex lives. Many attendees booed the bigotry; some, like Andrew Breitbart, fought the power with '80s-themed gay dance parties.

Perhaps fearing the attention that open disagreement on a pivotal social issue within the Republican Party would bring, the ACU took GOProud off the CPAC invitation list by 2012. The mixed message on LGBT issues of the past few years left Mitt Romney, a notorious waffler, confused as to which side to pander to. Romney, now the Republican nominee for president, hired Grenell, by then a seasoned Bush appointee, as his national security spokesman. Grenell lasted two weeks.

Initially, the Romney campaign accepted all the plaudits for having hired an openly gay man. But Grenell, reports later revealed, kept doggedly insisting on speaking out publicly on foreign policy—the job he was hired to do. Having a gay man on his staff, but not actually doing any serious work, was likely Romney's way of attempting to placate both sides of the CPAC-GOProud war. Reports differ on whether Romney pushed Grenell out of the position because of pressure from social conservative groups or if Grenell departed in protest, feeling muzzled in his post.

"I gathered Ric was frustrated that Team Romney wouldn't aggressively engage Obama on foreign policy. Ric was kept from talking to the press as a spokesman typically would. They seem to have decided to concede foreign policy to Obama, and therefore didn't need an aggressive spokesman," Christian Whiton, who worked in Bush's State Department and was thus familiar with Grenell for years, told *Politico* when Grenell resigned. "This confirms the worst of what people think of team Romney," Whiton lamented. "It seems in retrospect like Grenell was hired to check some diversity box, but was then kept in the closet because others were offended."

Grenell's resignation statement expressed frustration. "While I welcomed the challenge to confront President Obama's foreign policy failures and weak leadership on the world stage, my ability to speak clearly and forcefully on the issues has been greatly diminished by the hyper-partisan discussion of personal issues that sometimes comes from a presidential campaign," Grenell said. He added that Romney had given a "clear message to me that being openly gay was a non-issue for him and his team," which can be interpreted as either a gracious statement of appreciation or a parting shot to tarnish Romney's reputation with the people fighting behind the scenes to take Grenell out.

Grenell confirmed in a 2018 Breitbart News interview that the Romney campaign had told him, "You should stay silent until this blows over," referring to the controversy surrounding his appointment, and called it a "disastrous decision" and a "real leadership moment for a lot of people." The pressure to lend the Republican Party street cred with gay people and then immediately become invisible so as not to offend conservative sensibilities continued nearly uninterrupted for Grenell until Trump took over the party. A year after GOProud disbanded over yet another CPAC controversy, the conference invited and swiftly disinvited Grenell to speak.

The Trump era has brought redemption to Grenell, arguably the Republican whom the party has treated the worst in the past decade. Rather than offering him a ceremonial position and demanding he be silent, Trump has done the opposite; he promoted Grenell to highly influential positions, then handed him the biggest microphone. As ambassador to Germany, Grenell had the all-important job of pressuring delinquent, but prestigious, European nations like Germany and France to pay their share of NATO defense expenditures. He also leveraged his position to lead State Department initiatives to pressure nations to decriminalize homosexuality. He also sometimes took on some of the LGBT community's greatest enemies in work that also rose to the utmost importance in national security, such as leading the effort to get Germany to designate the Shiite group Hezbollah a terrorist organization and organizing the extradition of an elderly known Nazi found hiding out in the United States.

> **STEVE HILTON**: Just one thing on [Pete Buttigieg], putting aside policy disagreements, don't you think it's just great to see that you've got a guy there on the stage with his husband and it's normal—
> **TRUMP**: I think it's absolutely fine; I do.
> **HILTON**: But isn't it a sign of great progress in the country that that's just—
> **TRUMP**: Yeah, I think it's great. I think that's something that perhaps some people will have a problem with. I have no problem with it whatsoever, I think it's good.

In Trump's administration, Ambassador Grenell had the freedom to be openly gay and champion gay issues. But he was no token,

and was tasked with some of America's most important foreign policy issues. "I watched it from a front-row seat going from people privately telling me 'I'm with ya' to not being able to say it publicly or
there were times at Republican Conventions that if you were seen as
too good of a friend with Rick Grenell, well, you probably were gay,"
Grenell said of his rise in the party in the 2018 Breitbart interview.
"It's never been an issue for President Trump. He communicated
that very early on which is another reason I was wildly excited about
his candidacy."

So as to put an exclamation point on Grenell's story, Trump then
appointed him acting director of national intelligence, a cabinet-
level position. Rather than applauding a historic moment in LGBT
visibility in the country, CNN ran a column accusing Grenell of
being a "misogynist" with a "long history of nastiness," the claims
of which go uncorroborated.

Foreign Policy declared that Grenell's milestone achievement
was "the death of truth to power" because Grenell had been so effec-
tive in his previous job as ambassador to Germany—and the most
prominent LGBT ambassador in American history. *Foreign Policy*'s
gripe with Grenell was that he allegedly did not have the career
background for the job, a complaint the article itself obliterates with
the sentence: "In fairness, and as background, there is not exactly a
traditional director of national intelligence mold."

Bette Midler wrote a homophobic poem calling Grenell a
"goon" and accusing Senator Lindsey Graham (R-SC), whom Senator Mark Kirk (R-IL) famously called a "bro with no ho," of being
in love with him. Meanwhile, allegedly pro-LGBT organizations
like GLAAD completely ignored the achievement. The only article

tagged "Richard Grenell" on GLAAD's website complains that the Trump administration has not done enough for LGBT people in Uganda.

Sadly, for someone as confident in his identity as Grenell, a conservative who happens to be gay, the hate continues. But at least, thanks to Donald Trump, it's no longer coming from his own side.

7.

VIOLENT CRIME HAS FALLEN EVERY YEAR SINCE TRUMP TOOK OFFICE, AFTER RISING THE LAST TWO YEARS UNDER OBAMA

Violent crime spiked in 2015 and 2016 during Obama's last years in office. The number of murders in the United States spiked from 12,278 in 2014 to 15,195 in 2016.

That's a big jump, especially in light of how America has enjoyed falling crime rates for decades. Violent crime in 2016 jumped 59 percent from just a year earlier. In individual cities, the jump was even more stark. It increased "56 percent in Memphis, 61 percent in San Antonio, 44 percent in Louisville, 36 percent in Phoenix and 31 percent in Las Vegas," ABC News–owned data-analysis website FiveThirtyEight concluded based on figures compiled from official police data. "Taken together, those six cities accounted for 76 percent of the overall big city murder rise in 2016." According to FBI data released in September 2019, the rate of violent crimes in the U.S. has dropped by about 50 percent since the early 1990s, the high-water mark for violence in America.

Could the Obama crime wave be a blip on the radar, a statistical aberration that was unavoidable? I don't think so. And neither does political commentator and author Heather Mac Donald. She put the increase of violent crime directly on the shoulders of Obama and his outright antipathy toward law enforcement. Mac Donald also faults his support of anti-police groups like Black Lives Matter, a group that played a role in creating the Ferguson Effect, which describes the increase in crime as a result of police holding back in response to the Black Lives Matter movement. Mac Donald is the right person to comment on the Ferguson Effect, since she coined the term in a *Wall Street Journal* op-ed.

To wit, Mac Donald offers some insight on why violence spiked under Obama:

> **The reason for the current increase is what I have called the Ferguson Effect. Cops are backing off of proactive policing in high-crime minority neighborhoods, and criminals are becoming emboldened. Having been told incessantly by politicians, the media, and Black Lives Matter activists that they are bigoted for getting out of their cars and questioning someone loitering on a known drug corner at 2 AM, many officers are instead just driving by. Such stops are discretionary; cops don't have to make them. And when political elites demonize the police for just such proactive policing, we shouldn't be surprised when cops get the message and do less of it. Seventy-two percent of the nation's officers say that they and their colleagues are now less willing to stop and question**

**suspicious persons, according to a Pew Research poll
released in January 2016. The reason is the persistent
anti-cop climate.**

Former FBI director James Comey understood what was happening, too. Before he put all his energy into trying to prevent a
Donald Trump presidency, Comey said of the Ferguson Effect, "I
don't know whether that explains it entirely, but I do have a strong
sense that some part of the explanation is a chill wind that has blown
through American law enforcement over the last year."

Violent crime has fallen every year of the Trump presidency.
Now I know what you might be thinking. "So what? You just told us
it's fallen for decades!" I'm not trying to give Donald Trump credit
for the trend lasting nearly thirty years. But Trump has played a
role in the drop in violent crime. The data showed a 3.9 percent drop
in violent crimes from 2018, which doesn't sound all that exciting
until you put it in perspective: Violent crime in America hasn't been
at such a low level since 1971.

Mac Donald predicted that violent crime rates would improve
under Trump, returning the country to the trend line of fewer murders and other horrific crimes.

> The country has just elected a new president who
> understands that the false narrative about the police
> has led to the breakdown of law and order in inner
> cities. If the crime situation improves in the coming
> year, it will be because Black Lives Matter calum-
> nies no longer have an echo chamber in the White

House and because cops on the beat believe that they will now be supported for trying to restore order where informal social control has broken down.
—Heather Mac Donald, writing after the 2016 election

You already know Mac Donald was right. Trump obviously ended Black Lives Matter's connection to the White House. He also came out hard on the subject of supporting police instead of attacking them. Speaking to the International Association of Chiefs of Police, Trump made his intentions clear. "We understand that reducing crime begins with respecting law enforcement. For too many years, we have watched politicians escalate political attacks on our courageous police officers," he said. And in true President Trump fashion, he took the opportunity to point out how wrongheaded his political opponents are. "I've never seen it more than over the last few years. It's disgraceful. They also make it more dangerous for police, and it must stop, and it must stop now."

The Trump administration stopped the Ferguson Effect in its tracks. The beneficiaries of the attitude change in the White House have been black Americans, especially, and the poor residents of crime-ridden neighborhoods and inner cities. I agree with Mac Donald that the reversal of the Ferguson Effect is the best explanation for how Trump has restored the country's downward trend in crime, but many other policies are likely to have contributed as well. For example, Trump has achieved record low unemployment levels for blacks and Hispanics. A young man, of any ethnic background, with a job is less likely to turn to crime.

All signs point to violent crime continuing to fall under President Trump. While the chronically shameless media and Democrats will never admit it, steadily decreasing violent crime is a win for the everyday Americans in cities like Detroit, St. Louis, and (hopefully one day) Baltimore.

8.

FARMER WAGES GREW AT THE FASTEST PACE IN TWO DECADES

America has the honor of being one of the few nations that serve as a breadbasket for the world, producing an overwhelming amount of grains, produce, and livestock that feed the planet. The United States' farmworkers are a crucial part of making America a dominant agricultural force in the world. And President Donald Trump's policies have ushered in record-level wages for farmworkers.

The U.S. Department of Agriculture (USDA) Economic Research Service reported in February 2019 that the increase in real (inflation-adjusted) wages for farmworkers from 2014 to 2018 rose from "$12.00 per hour to $13.25 per hour, an increase of 10.4 percent." The USDA concluded, "This increase in the real wage for farm labor is the fastest experienced over a 4-year period during the past two decades." The USDA found that growth in farmworkers' wages grew faster than the increase in nonfarm wages. The USDA Economic Research Service noted, "Over the period 2014–18, the real hourly wage for all nonsupervisory production workers outside agriculture rose from $21.90 to $22.97 (in 2018 dollars), an increase of 3.5 percent." That federal agency also reported that "in 2018, the farm wage was 58.5 percent of the nonfarm wage, compared with 54.8 percent in 2014."

Data revealed that regional farm wages in certain areas also grew faster than the national rate. The agency noted, "Regional wage data show that over the past four years, farm wages rose faster than the national rate of 10.4 percent in several regions: California (15.6 percent), Mountain Region I (Idaho, Montana, and Wyoming, 13.9 percent), Pacific (Oregon and Washington, 13.9 percent), Appalachian Region I (North Carolina and Virginia, 11.7 percent), the Southern Plains (Oklahoma and Texas, 11.2 percent), and Northeast Region I (Connecticut, Massachusetts, Maine, New Hampshire, New York, Rhode Island, and Vermont, 10.7 percent)."

The FDA found that, as of November 2019, American farm wage rates grew to as high as $15 per hour and roughly $14.50 per hour for field and livestock workers. The dynamism of the Trump economy has also spurred a tight labor market, which has increased farm wages and led to farms hiring more Americans compared to foreign immigrant workers who'd often work for far less pay. The FDA suggested that other indicators of tighter farm labor included that agricultural companies hired fewer nonimmigrant, foreign-born workers through the H-2A Temporary Agricultural Workers visa program and that there was a decrease in the number of illegal immigrants from Mexico working on America's farms.

"Many U.S. growers of labor-intensive crops have long relied on farmworkers from Mexico, including some workers who are not legally authorized to be employed in the United States," the FDA noted. "In the mid-20th century, as the U.S. workforce continued its long-run transition away from farm work, U.S. growers turned to Mexico to bolster the supply of farm labor. During much of the latter half of the twentieth century, workers from rural Mexico provided a plentiful supply of farm labor to the United States at relatively low wages."

The success of Trump's economy and the shortage of illegal migrant workers means that agricultural CEOs are increasingly utilizing labor-saving machinery and raising farmworkers' wages, according to a November 2018 *New York Times* report. Furthermore, the American farm labor supply shortage meant that California farmers had to hike wages for American workers and automate their farming. A California Bureau Federation survey released in May 2019 found that 86 percent of farmers said that they had increased wages to attract workers. "Farmers are becoming more reliant on technology due to rising wages and increased farm employee scarcity," the survey noted.

> Farmers in California as well as throughout the United States have been forthright about the fact that they rely on a largely immigrant workforce. Our survey shows that farmers face new challenges related to employee availability. It offers insight into the means farmers use to adjust to this reality. Farmers are paying higher wages, and their farming practices are changing in response to reduced employee availability.
>
> —California Bureau Federation survey

A March 2019 *New York Times* report detailed how a labor shortage, coupled with Immigration and Customs Enforcement (ICE) raids on dairy farms that were filled with illegal immigrant laborers, has led to improved working conditions on American dairy farms and saw farm owners hiking wages. The *New York Times* noted:

> **Without a legal alternative to informal migrant labor, the competition between dairy farms to retain migrant workers is so fierce that farm owners, once notorious for underpaying and mistreating workers, are now improving working conditions and wages to entice employees to stay on their farms, workers said.**
>
> **Victor Cortez is an immigrant who has worked on a dairy farm in western New York for eighteen years. A few years ago, farm owners "wouldn't let us leave the farm," he said, adding, "They wouldn't pay us as much as they promised they would."**
>
> **"But the good thing about it now," he said, "is that we get paid more, and this farmer is good to me."**

Center for Immigration Studies (CIS) Director Mark Krikorian has said that rather than have American dairy farms rely on cheap foreign labor, the American government should provide loans for smaller dairy farmers to invest in robots and machines to do the work more efficiently and without having to hire illegal immigrant labor.

Senior White House officials have touted the tight American labor market. White House senior adviser Ivanka Trump said that the American legal immigration system must strike a balance between attracting talent and labor, but must not displace American workers.

"Immigration, I think it actually would have bipartisan agreement . . . that it needs to be overhauled and become relevant to both the jobs and the skills we need to attract to continue to grow and thrive, but it can't displace the investment that needs to be made and the core skills of marginalized Americans," Ms. Trump said at CES 2020 in January.

At CPAC in February 2020, she said, "Low unemployment rates are forcing employers to get creative . . . [and] wages are higher."

"We were saying that our national policies are achieving the desired goal that everyone wants, which is decreasing income inequality," she went on. "So there's a lot of talk about inequality, but this president's policies—because more people are working than before, because wages are rising, and because they're proportionately rising for the lower-income earners—income inequality is decreasing for the first time in over twelve years."

9.

PRESIDENT TRUMP LEGALIZES HEMP AND CBD OIL, A BOON FOR PATIENTS AND FARMERS

In December 2018, President Donald Trump signed Congress's omnibus Farm Bill into law, which legalized hemp and cannabidiol (CBD) oil. Senate Majority Leader Mitch McConnell (R-KY) helped push for the legalization of hemp in the 2018 Farm Bill. The measure, which made it possible for farmers to purchase crop insurance for hemp, helped eliminate some of the risks for farmers to expand into the burgeoning market. The bill also allowed for hemp to be sold across state lines. Brett Kelman described hemp in the *Tennessean*: "Hemp, which is closely related to marijuana but has no psychoactive effect, has been classified as a controlled substance under federal law for decades. The Farm Bill removes this designation and reclassifies hemp as an agricultural product, legally distancing hemp from pot, which is still illegal to grow in most states."

The president touted the bill as a "tremendous victory for the American farmer," cheering the proposal for the rare bipartisan support it engendered and even congratulating Democrats who helped craft the bill. "I'll probably have to deny that someday, but I won't do that because you worked really, really hard," Trump said.

Farmers are now free to grow hemp, which produces a fiber that's used to manufacture clothing, rope, and building materials. They can also harvest hemp into CBD. The legalization of hemp and, subsequently, CBD oil will help the industry get access to financial services such as bank loans, credit cards, and lines of credit, which, until Trump, it has had to survive without.

Jonathan Miller, an expert on hemp law, told the *Tennessean* in December 2018, "Everybody who has been in the industry before now has taken a risk, and frankly, I think it's proven to be a wise risk. But this Farm Bill, more than anything, takes away that risk. . . . There is no longer going to [be] the specter of the DEA coming in and arresting people."

The Associated Press (AP) reported in November 2019 that the legalization of industrial hemp and CBD had sparked interest from both small farmers and larger, more industrial agricultural companies. The industry could grow by more than 500 percent by 2025, according to some estimates. The United States is the largest hemp-importing country, meaning that American farmers can now compete with countries that have long dominated the hemp and CBD markets. Market research firm Brightfield Group estimated that U.S. CBD sales in 2018 reached $600 million and could increase by more than 700 percent to $5 billion in 2020. Brightfield's research found that the market could grow to $23 billion within the next four years.

Hemp can't get you high. For decades, federal law did not differentiate hemp from other cannabis plants, all of which were effectively made illegal in

> 1937 under the Marihuana Tax Act and formally
> made illegal in 1970 under the Controlled Sub-
> stances Act—the latter banned cannabis of any
> kind.
>
> —The Brookings Institute

"This business has exploded in one year with the passage of the new farm bill," says Jeanine Davis, a specialist for herbs, organics, and specialty crops at North Carolina State University, in an interview with the *New York Times*. "After thirty-one years in the business, this is fun to see this kind of growth. I thought the hops market was going to be big, but this is much greater."

Blake Butler, executive director of the North Carolina Hemp Association, told the *Times*, "The demand in the CBD market has grown so quickly that we aren't really looking right now at the long game for hemp fiber and grain. There are huge opportunities on the horizon, particularly for fiber."

The legalization of hemp and CBD has also allowed doctors to explore CBD's potential medical uses. James MacKillop, co-director of McMaster University's Michael G. DeGroote Center for Medicinal Cannabis Research in Hamilton, Ontario, said, "It's promising in a lot of different therapeutic avenues because it's relatively safe." The *New York Times* noted in 2019 that the FDA has approved CBD extracts such as Epidiolex to treat "rare seizure disorders." Other studies have found that patients with "generalized social anxiety" could benefit from CBD.

Our armed services are also getting in on the action. The Department of Veterans Affairs (VA) is funding a study to see how CBD oil could prove therapeutic for soldiers returning from war and suffering from post-traumatic stress disorder. Mallory Loflin, an assistant adjunct professor at the University of California and the study's principal investigator, told the *New York Times*, "Our top therapies attempt to break the association between reminders of the trauma and the fear response. We think that CBD, at least in animal models, can help that process happen a lot faster."

CBD could also potentially be used as a sleep aid. MacKillop explained, "If you are looking for new treatments for sleep, that may be a clue." Sâmia Joca, a fellow at the Aarhus Institute of Advanced Studies in Denmark, told the *New York Times*, "Surprisingly, CBD seems to act faster than conventional antidepressants."

10.

TRUMP AUTHORIZED THE LARGEST WILDERNESS PRESERVATION EXPANSION IN A DECADE

The American left has often smeared President Trump as having no regard for how his policies impact the environment. He's painted as a president willing to rip up every environmental regulation to the detriment of America's natural beauty. For instance, the left often cites Trump tapping former Oklahoma attorney general Scott Pruitt and former coal lobbyist Andrew Wheeler to lead the EPA as evidence of his anti-environmental agenda. "Trump has savaged the environment. The planet cannot afford a second term," read a headline in *The Guardian*. "Trump's Latest Environmental Rollback Is a Middle Finger to Common Sense," screamed a *Huffington Post* headline. While they're so busy endlessly attacking the president's eco agenda, which hones in on removing arduous regulations, the left seldom mention that President Trump signed the most significant wilderness bill in a decade.

In March 2020, President Trump signed into law a wide-ranging public lands bill, otherwise known as the John D. Dingell Jr. Conservation, Management, and Recreation Act. The act serves as the most substantial public lands bill signed in a decade, receiving large bipartisan majorities in the House and Senate.

Former president Barack Obama had signed the last major conservationist bill in March 2009, when he backed a bill that established two million acres of new wilderness across the West, including 710,00 acres across the Sierra Nevada, Angeles National Forest, and the California desert. Congress named the Trump-backed bill after former Michigan Democrat Representative John Dingell, who died in February 2019 at the age of ninety-two. Dingell, a lifelong outdoorsman, crafted some of the nation's landmark conservation laws during his fifty-nine years in the House of Representatives and helped designate the Detroit River International Wildlife Refuge.

"That's his love. That's what he spent his life doing," Representative Debbie Dingell (D-MI), John Dingell's widow, said. "I think he would be stunned." The Trump-signed bill adds 1.3 million acres of new wilderness to the public lands and permanently reauthorizes the Land and Water Conservation Fund (LWCF), which supports conservation and outdoor recreation nationwide. The legislation also designates roughly 700,000 acres of recreation and conservation areas. The LWCF's authorization expired in the fall of 2018 after Congress failed to agree on the language to extend the bill.

Representative Dingell said that her late husband spent more than two decades to get permanent authorization for the fund. "This will permanently protect our outdoors and natural resources for decades," she said in March 2019.

The LWCF has more than 42,000 state and local projects nationwide since Congress first authorized the program in 1964.

John D. Dingell Jr. Conservation, Management, and Recreation Act

The new legislation establishes three new monuments for the National Park Service and two others for the Forest Service and Bureau of Land Management to administer, including:

- The Medgar and Myrlie Evers Home National Monument in Mississippi
- The Mill Springs National Cemetery and Camp Nelson National Monument in Kentucky
- The former Saint Francis Dam site in southern California. Four hundred and thirty-one people died when the dam collapsed in 1928 near Santa Clarita.
- The Jurassic National Monument in Utah

It also establishes 375,000 acres of new wilderness in the Mojave Desert, an area that is roughly thirteen times the size of San Francisco. The bill also enlarges the Death Valley National Park by 35,929 acres and the Joshua Tree National Park by 4,518 acres.

Those concerned with protecting nature have praised the bill's passage into law. Geary Hund, executive director of the Mojave

Desert Land Trust, said in March 2019, "This legislation is a huge win for conservation." He added, "It ensures that some of the most important natural and cultural resources in the Mojave Desert will be protected and connected in perpetuity."

Jamie Williams, president of the Wilderness Society, said in March 2019, "This is a strong start and an opportunity to turn the corner after two years of backsliding by the Trump Administration and its allies on Capitol Hill. By passing this momentous bill, Congress has embraced the conservation and protection of our nation's wildlands and waters."

Republicans, such as Senator Steve Daines (R-MT), have contended that conservatives can and should work to protect America's natural beauty without resorting to harmful and onerous policies such as the Green New Deal and carbon taxes. "What a great day for Montana, a great day for America," Daines said at the signing ceremony for the legislation in March 2019. "I just came back from the West Wing of the White House, the Oval Office, where I witnessed President Trump sign the lands package. In fact, here's one of the pens from the signing ceremony that I keep as a souvenir. This permanently reauthorizes LWCF and signs into law the Yellowstone Gateway Protection Act, protecting a very important part of Montana there in Paradise Valley. Congratulations."

The Montana *Flathead Beacon* profiled Daines in 2015. The paper called him a "Teddy Roosevelt" Republican and a "conservative conservationist" who fights for protecting conservative values and America's natural beauty at the same time. Indeed, President Trump and Republican lawmakers are not content with that victory; they hope to expand conservation efforts to preserve America's natural beauty for future generations. Now, Senators Daines and Cory

Gardner (R-CO) have moved to pass legislation that would provide full funding of the LWCF and address the $12 billion maintenance backlog in the nation's parks.

Daines and Gardner announced in March 2020 that they have secured President Trump's support for bipartisan action to address these conservation issues. "We are proud to announce that we have secured the President's support to provide full and permanent funding for the Land and Water Conservation Fund and address the maintenance backlog at our national parks, and the bipartisan group here today demonstrates the strong backing these programs benefit from in Congress," said Gardner. "The LWCF supports projects in Colorado and all across our country at no cost to the taxpayer, and fighting every year to figure out how much money the program will receive doesn't provide the long-term planning certainty that our outdoor and conservation community deserves. I thank President Trump and Leader McConnell for their support and look forward to getting full, permanent funding signed into law."

"This is a historic day for conservation, Montana, and this nation. I am proud to stand here today and announce that after my meeting with President Trump, Senator Gardner, and Leader McConnell, we have the support we need to provide full and mandatory funding for LWCF and address the maintenance backlog at our national parks," said Daines. "For Montanans, protecting our public lands is about protecting our way of life. That's why I've made it my top priority since coming to Congress to fight for LWCF and our parks. I look forward to getting this historic conservation victory across the finish line for future generations of Montanans."

11.

THE FAMOUS "MUSLIM BAN" EXCLUDED 87 PERCENT OF THE WORLD'S MUSLIMS

"We need your help. I'm basically here to ask for your help. Because it's really scary to be a Muslim right now. Super scary," the British actor and rapper Riz Ahmed pleaded with fellow Hollywood fixtures during a speech at an event in June 2019. "I often wonder if this is going to be the year they round us up, if this is the year they're going to put Trump's Muslim registry into action, if this is going to be the year they ship us all off . . . I think lives are quite literally at stake here," he added.

Ahmed's panicked warning about "Trump's Muslim registry" reportedly received a standing ovation. No one questioned the registry's existence. Few reporting on Ahmed's speech even highlighted the strange conspiracy theory, instead applauding Ahmed for urging Hollywood to tell more Muslim stories.

The "Muslim registry" is one of the more eccentric bits of disinformation celebrity leftists and politicians have spread about President Donald Trump. It is a conspiracy theory that has been bouncing around since at least 2017. Trump ordered the government to make a list of every Muslim in America to have on hand for the day he

decides to deport them all—regardless of where they were born—
the theory goes. The conspiracy theory never quite gets around to
what to do about recent converts to or from the religion, or if Trump
ever updated the list since the mainstream media made it up.

It is far from the last falsehood that Trump's opponents have
spread with the intention to alienate Muslims from the president.
There are few Democrats at this point who have not accused Trump
of banning all Muslim immigration or travel into the United States.
The famous "Muslim ban" excluded 87 percent of the world's Muslims and included North Korea and Venezuela. The Council for
American-Islamic Relations (CAIR), an unindicted co-conspirator
in one of America's largest jihadist financing trials, routinely refers
to Trump as Islamophobic.

What the attacks and convoluted accusations fail to mention is
that President Trump has prioritized the Muslim world in his foreign policy and welcomed its representatives to the White House.
Trump made his first trip abroad as president to the heart of the
Muslim world, Saudi Arabia, home to the holy cities of Mecca and
Medina. The Trump White House has opened its doors to Uighurs,
Rohingya, and other Muslim ethnic minorities facing genocide for
their faith. In targeting the leaders of some of the world's premier
jihadist outfits, he has avenged thousands of Muslims killed for not
being the right kind of Muslim, or not Muslim enough.

Addressing the Muslim world in 2017 from Riyadh, the capital
of Saudi Arabia, during his first trip as president abroad, Trump
made clear that prioritizing the elimination of radical Islamist terrorism was not a policy meant to antagonize the Muslim world as a
whole. On the contrary, it was a policy meant to save Muslim lives.

President Trump's Speech to the Arab Islamic American Summit

America is a sovereign nation and our first priority is always the safety and security of our citizens. We are not here to lecture—we are not here to tell other people how to live, what to do, who to be, or how to worship. Instead, we are here to offer partnership—based on shared interests and values—to pursue a better future for us all . . .

The nations of Europe have also endured un-speakable horror. So too have the nations of Africa and even South America. . . . But, in sheer numbers, the deadliest toll has been exacted on the innocent people of Arab, Muslim, and Middle Eastern nations. They have borne the brunt of the killings and the worst of the destruction in this wave of fanatical violence. Some estimates hold that more than 95 percent of the victims of terrorism are themselves Muslim.

Trump vowed to play his part in eradicating radical Islamic terrorism, working with whoever would accept his offer in the region. Saudi Arabia was among the first and most eager partners. Crown Prince Mohammad bin Salman applauded Trump as a "true friend of Muslims who will serve the Muslim World in an unimaginable manner."

For most presidents, such an endorsement from the custodian of two of the holiest cities in Islam would result in some praise. For Trump, it just got him called a "bitch."

During his visit to Riyadh, Trump, the Saudis, and Egyptian president Abdel Fattah el-Sisi inaugurated the Global Center for Combating Extremist Ideology, heralded as a major first step in fighting back against an Islamic State on the ascent and an increasingly belligerent Shiite Iran. Today, the only thing most people remember about that announcement was the inexplicable presence of a giant, glowing orb, which Sisi, Trump, and King Salman of Saudi Arabia held in their palms, one hand per head of state.

The orb ignited a fire under the seats of the American officials responsible for taking out our country's enemies in the last four years. Allied with Saudi Arabia and Egypt, two Sunni nations, it is perhaps not surprising that Trump made the decision as commander in chief to eliminate one of the most prolific murderers of Sunni Muslims in the world: Major General Qasem Soleimani, the head of the Quds Force, Iran's Islamic Revolutionary Guard Corps (IRGC) external terrorism unit. Trump first designated the IRGC a foreign terrorist organization—an unprecedented step, as the IRGC is also a formal wing of a sovereign state's armed forces—in April 2019. By January of the next year, Soleimani was dead.

Soleimani was a strategist responsible for killing countless Sunni Muslims, and his forces were responsible for planting roadside bombs in Iraq and Syria. The reason Trump chose to conduct an airstrike against Soleimani was the death of a Muslim American.

Nawres Waleed Hamid, an Iraqi immigrant from California, was working as a civilian contractor near the city of Kirkuk when the

Hezbollah Brigades, a militia with close ties to Soleimani, launched a rocket attack at U.S. troops in the area. The U.S. swiftly retaliated with a rocket attack of its own that spurred allies of the brigades to attack the U.S. embassy in Baghdad, spray-painting "Soleimani is our commander" on its walls. Trump then decided to pull the trigger.

Sunni Islamists who view Trump, and America generally, as the enemy could not help but celebrate that Soleimani would no longer torment fellow Muslims. "He was a hero according to the Shiite world, yet according to the overwhelming majority of the Muslim world, he was a war criminal murderer," Ibrahim Karagül, an Islamist anti-American commentator in Turkey, wrote. "The U.S. having killed Soleimani . . . will not absolve him."

Lest anyone accuse Trump of eliminating only Shiite terrorists, the president also approved a mission to capture the deadliest Sunni terrorist of his time: Abu Bakr al-Baghdadi, identified as the caliph of the Islamic State (ISIS). Al-Baghdadi controlled much of Iraq and Syria between 2014 and 2017, killing tens of thousands of Muslims, including Shiites whom the Islamic State considered infidels; moderates who rejected ISIS's extreme ideology; anyone suspected of homosexuality, adultery, conversion to other religions, or disloyalty; and Kurdish Muslims on the front lines of the caliphate.

The deaths piled up fast during ISIS's reign of terror: nearly 10,000 killed in the first eight months of 2014 alone, according to the United Nations, when ISIS announced the establishment of its caliphate. By the time of al-Baghdadi's suicide, surrounded by U.S. troops and his wives, death tolls in Iraq and Syria were in the hundreds of thousands. While many civilians were victims of Shiite militias and Syrian president Bashar al-Assad, the Islamic State is widely considered the deadliest group in the recent history of the region.

Off the battlefield, President Trump has used the State Department to confront regimes for repression of their minority Muslim populations. Nowhere has the State Department been more vocal in defense of Muslims than in China, where the Communist Party has established concentration camps it refers to as "vocational centers" for Muslims, most of whom are ethnic Uighurs. Even before news of the camps surfaced, from State Department reports in 2017, the first religious freedom reports in the Trump era exposed Chinese policies used "to extract unpaid labor, conduct indoctrination sessions, and closely monitor and restrict the movements of Uighurs."

In July 2019, Trump welcomed a group of advocates for religious freedom to the White House, including representatives of the Uighur community. Among them was Jewher Ilham, whose father, a Uighur scholar, was sentenced to life in prison in China in 2016 for speaking out against communist repression of his people. In welcoming her, Trump offered his platform to the Uighur people to condemn abuses against both them and Muslims generally in China.

Trump has also repeatedly offered support to the Rohingya Muslims of Myanmar, who were also in attendance at the July meeting. The Buddhist government of Myanmar has largely spent the past five years trying to eliminate ethnic Rohingya Muslims from the country, unleashing genocidal policies like top-down starvation that have forced over a million to flee for their lives to neighboring Bangladesh and other states, according to the United Nations.

In 2017, when that number was still 600,000, Trump mentioned the issue at that year's East Asia Summit. He pressured Myanmar to end its genocidal policies and dispatched then–Secretary of State Rex Tillerson to the country. A year later, Vice President Mike Pence kept on the pressure in defense of the Rohingya.

"The Rohingya were victimized by nothing less than ethnic cleansing: extrajudicial killings, rapes, tortures, beatings, arbitrary arrests, displacement, destruction of property—all driven by intolerance and sectarian hatred," Pence announced to the world during that year's Religious Freedom Ministerial, an annual State Department tradition when top diplomats from around the world are invited to come together to tackle religious persecution.

Last year, Trump welcomed Rohingya representatives to the Oval Office, just as Secretary of State Mike Pompeo announced new sanctions to pressure Myanmar to stop persecuting the ethnic minority. The sanctions were the latest in years of economic measures corresponding with public statements in defense of Myanmar's Muslims.

While Trump has invested heavily in policies defending the human rights of Muslims and eliminating threats to worshipping freely under Islam, he has not by any means come close to solving every issue on his desk when he took office. Perhaps nowhere is that more glaringly obvious than in Africa. Crushing the Islamic State in its territory in Syria and Iraq triggered a tsunami of terrorists flooding faraway lands with established ISIS affiliates seeking refuge and new battlefields to plague. In western Africa, many jihadists have found a home with Boko Haram, the Nigerian Sunni jihadist outfit, which pledged allegiance to al-Baghdadi in 2015.

Boko Haram rose to international prominence before Trump's tenure, in 2014, when the group abducted about 300 girls from a secondary school in Chibok, northern Nigeria. Unlike many of the Middle East's jihadist groups, it has separated itself from the pack by targeting Christian schools. The group's name roughly translates to "Western education is sin" in the Hausa language. They kidnap Christian girls and force them to convert to Islam. Many girls endure slavery, rape, and torture. Those successfully indoctrinated go on to serve as suicide bombers, some as young as age seven. These girls are sought by Boko Haram to use as suicide bombers because they look so innocent.

Boko Haram often targets Shiite mosques or religious events too, making the group an active threat to Nigeria's Muslim communities as well as its Christians. Boko Haram also operates in heavily Muslim northeastern Nigeria, and recently spread into Muslim communities in Chad, Cameroon, Niger, and Burkina Faso.

After the fall of the ISIS caliphate in 2019, militias of Iraq and Syria stopped cooperating and once again started fighting with one another. As the Middle East struggled for stability, international observers began to warn that Boko Haram was building a proto-state in its native northern Nigeria.

In light of growing concerns that radical Islamic elements are taking over larger territories in the region, President Trump has expanded cooperation with the government of Nigeria and its neighbors. He has welcomed Nigerian president Muhammadu Buhari to the White House and continued offering aid against Boko Haram to the country. U.S. soldiers remain in nations like Niger fighting jihadist groups, often triggering outrage in the U.S. media. (Of course, if Trump hints at seeking a way out for those troops, the media decries his ignorance and disrespect for African allies.)

Yet, supporting shady characters like Buhari has proven to be a mistake. Buhari declared Boko Haram defeated in 2015 and has done so, falsely, every year since. In 2019, his soldiers began insisting that the Boko Haram continuing to kidnap girls and use them as suicide bombers was a different group—Islamic State West Africa Province (ISWAP), and that Boko Haram no longer existed. This is true in only the most technical sense: Boko Haram changed its name to ISWAP in 2015, but there is no evidence ISWAP is made up of a new group of terrorists or that Boko Haram veterans no longer remain on the battlefield. The White House, perhaps overloaded with international crises, has done little in public to hold Buhari and his administration accountable for this shameless buffoonery. It also has to face a few other concerning actors: Cameroon's President Paul Biya, who is violently eradicating his country's English speakers from the general population, and Niger's Idriss Deby, who changes presidential term limit rules like he changes his clothes and is expected to hold sixth and seventh terms in office since taking power in 1990. But the crisis offers ample opportunity to expand on what has been a tremendously successful foreign policy during Trump's first term to make the world a safer place for Muslims.

12.

LATINOS ARE NEARLY ONE-THIRD MORE LIKELY TO START A BUSINESS UNDER TRUMP THAN THEY WERE UNDER OBAMA

Latinos who own a business saw their average income soar 46.5 percent in 2019, an increase that represented a whopping $152,224. "Meanwhile, the number of credit applications from Latino-owned businesses increased by 23 percent over the past 12 months," read a report from the small business financing platform Biz2Credit, which published its study after examining financial information submitted by 3,000 Latino-owned businesses.

The number of Latino-owned businesses has exploded in recent years. Data from the Census Bureau Survey of Business Owners shows that there were 3.3 million Latino-owned businesses in 2012. That number jumped to over 4 million, according to a 2017 report. Today, nearly one in four new businesses are Latino-owned. "These businesses contribute over $700 billion to the American economy annually," according to a United States Joint Economic Committee report. "The rate of new entrepreneurs in 2017 was also much higher for Latinos than for any other racial group—Latinos are 1.7 times more likely to start businesses." One in four Latino-owned businesses are owned by women, the report also found.

> White House Council of Economic Advisers chairman Kevin Hassett observed in 2018 that business creation in America hit its highest level in recorded history. The trend, data shows, is being driven by Latinos who are nearly one-third more likely to start a business than they were in 2013 and are today two-thirds more likely to start a business than their white counterparts.

A 2019 Bank of America Hispanic Small Business Owner Spotlight report found that nearly 90 percent of Hispanic entrepreneurs planned to expand their business that year. Another 79 percent said they planned to expand their business over the next five years, versus just 55 percent for all other business owners. Over 50 percent of Latino entrepreneurs said they planned to hire new workers. Another 25 percent of non-Latino business owners said they planned to fill new job openings.

Over the last two decades, Hispanics have solidified themselves as the most entrepreneurial demographic in America. Latinos are starting new businesses at three times the national average. The wave of Latino entrepreneurship in recent years has likely been spurred by President Trump's deregulation agenda and pro-business policies, particularly the Tax Cuts and Jobs Act, which the president signed into law in 2017. This law includes several provisions that targeted entrepreneurs ready to take risks, hire more people, purchase new equipment, and increase wages. It also created a 20 percent small business tax deduction. "Fifty-eight percent cite the policy as a game-changer for small businesses overall, while 63 percent say it's made them more optimistic about their own business's outlook," read a Bank of America semiannual survey of 1,000 small business owners across the country.

The tax law also included measures to reduce the regulatory burden for small businesses, of which there are more than 30 million in America. Small business owners spend on average more than $83,000 on regulatory compliance costs in the first year of operation, according to a 2017 survey from the Washington-based National Small Business Association (NSBA), which queried 1,000 business owners. "The impact of regulatory burden cannot be overstated: more than one-third have held off on business investment due to uncertainty on a pending regulation, and more than half have held off on hiring a new employee due to regulatory burdens," said NSBA Chair Pedro Alfonso and President and CEO Todd McCracken.

It's no wonder then that roughly half of surveyed small business owners told the National Federation of Independent Business in 2017 that regulations are a "very serious" or "somewhat serious" problem. Confusion over how to remain compliant also creates a time-killing headache for small firms that don't have the benefit of a robust accounting staff.

And regulations hit small businesses harder than medium-sized and large corporations, the Small Business Administration (SBA) data finds. "Considering all federal regulations, all sectors of the

U.S. economy, and all firm sizes, federal regulations cost $8,086 per employee per year in 2008," according to a study from the SBA. "For firms with fewer than 20 employees, the cost is $10,585 per employee per year. The cost is $7,454 in medium-sized firms, and $7,755 in large firms."

To wit, in his first three years in office, President Trump signed sixteen pieces of deregulation legislation estimated to increase annual incomes by more than $40 billion. The Trump administration estimates that it cut eight and a half regulations for every new rule. "President Trump's deregulatory efforts have already slashed regulatory costs by nearly $50 billion, with savings reaching $220 billion once major actions are fully implemented. The Trump Administration's deregulatory efforts will help save American households an estimated $3,100 each year," the White House claims.

13.

UNDER TRUMP, BLUE-COLLAR WORKERS ENJOYED THREE TIMES THE WAGE GROWTH OF THE TOP 1 PERCENT OF HOUSEHOLDS

Blue-collar or working-class Americans propelled President Trump into the White House in 2016, abandoning a Democratic party that had been their long-established home. Blue-collar voters (particularly white working-class Americans with no college degree) were one-third of the electorate in 2016. They pulled the lever for Trump by a margin of 37 percentage points. The sledgehammer that Trump used to destroy the so-called Democratic Blue Wall was handed to him by Hillary Clinton. She campaigned very little in the industrial Midwest. She avoided Wisconsin for months before the election, allowing Trump to put that state in the Republican column for the first time since 1984; Clinton also spent little time in Michigan and lost there by fewer than 11,000 votes. Although she campaigned heavily in Pennsylvania, Trump trounced her there, too. Donald Trump also received 43 percent support from union households, the highest margin for a Republican since 1988.

Many of these people have found themselves benefiting from the America First economic dynamism agenda that Trump repeatedly promised on the campaign trail. By 2018, a blue-collar boom was in full bloom. Blue-collar jobs in mining, manufacturing, and construction grew 3.3 percent, the fastest rate since 1984, between July 2017 and July 2018, the *Washington Post* noted. Many of the 656,000 blue-collar jobs added in that time frame arrived in the same small towns and rural areas the president picked up in 2016. "Rural employment grew at an annualized rate of 5.1 percent in the first quarter. Smaller metro areas grew 5 percent. That's significantly larger than the 4.1 percent growth seen in large urban areas that recovered earlier from the Great Recession, according to an analysis by the Brookings Institution's Metropolitan Policy Program of a separate set of Labor Department data released on Wednesday," the *Washington Post* reported. Workers were also taking home fatter paychecks. Wages and salaries jumped 3.1 percent in the third quarter of 2018. It was the largest increase since the end of the Great Recession.

By January 2020, President Trump was taking a victory lap. "Under the Trump economy, the lowest-paid earners are reaping the biggest, fastest, and largest gains. This is a blue-collar boom," a campaigning President Trump told a packed crowd in Wisconsin. "They don't like telling you that," he said, pointing to the elite media cameras at the back of the room. "Under my administration, the growth in net worth for the bottom half of wage earners has increased fifteen times more than under the three previous administrations. That's pretty amazing because they keep saying, 'Oh, the rich you getting richer.' Well, the poor are doing the best they've ever done. Earnings for the bottom ten percent are rising faster than earnings for the top ten percent, proportionately."

Indeed, earnings for the bottom 25 percent of workers, who account for 82 percent of the population, rose 4.5 percent from November 2018 to November 2019, according to data published by the Federal Reserve Bank of Atlanta. That's the highest since July 2008. Some of that increase was jolted by a slew of states that increased their minimum wage. Other states have raised pay as a means to adjust for inflation. Still, the economic gains working Americans have reaped in the first few years of Trump's tenure go against the prevailing wisdom that warned of economic calamity if he assumed office. They also betray the narrative that Trump's policies would only benefit the mega-wealthy.

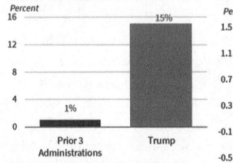

Growth in Real Net Worth of the Bottom 50 Percent

Sources: Federal Reserve Board; Bureau of Economic Analysis; CEA calculations.
Note: The lighter bar represents the average annual growth across previous administrations' expansion periods.

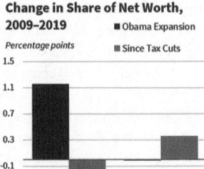

Change in Share of Net Worth, 2009–2019   ■ Obama Expansion   ■ Since Tax Cuts

Sources: Federal Reserve Board; CEA calculations.
Note: The lighter bars represent the thirty quarter change from 2009:Q3 to 2016:Q4.

> According to the White House Council of Economic Advisers, the net worth held by the bottom 50 percent of households has increased by 47 percent, more than three times the rate of increase for the top 1 percent of households. Under President Trump, real take home pay for the typical middle-class family has increased by roughly $5,000. And, at more than $66,000, real median household income is now at the highest level ever recorded.

The president's policies have also helped close the historically disheartening racial wealth gap. Average wage growth for black Americans has outpaced wage growth for white Americans, according to data from the Bureau of Labor Statistics.

14.

THE DEMOCRATS BEGAN CALLING FOR TRUMP'S IMPEACHMENT MONTHS BEFORE HE WAS THE REPUBLICAN NOMINEE

The plot to impeach Donald Trump was a fantasy being debated by congresspeople, pundits, and the press as early as March 2016, months before he won the Republican nomination. "Impeach Trump," screamed a March 2, 2016 *New York Daily News* headline. The article declared that "It's not too early to start" impeachment proceedings against Trump. Democrats in Congress concurred. Former representative Alan Grayson (D-FL) told *Politico* that month that Trump building a wall along the U.S.-Mexico border could be grounds for impeachment.

The *Politico* article from which Grayson is quoted is a peerless piece of work. In it, the D.C. publication's senior policy reporter Darren Samuelsohn dreamed up the hysterical scenario under which a Trump impeachment would easily garner support from both House and Senate Republicans. The *"Politico* time machine" takes readers to the summer of 2017. Trump has declared martial law in Detroit, Chicago, New York, "and other neighborhoods with large Muslim population" centers, which are being patrolled by the National Guard. Rumors swirl about Muslims being captured and shipped off to "Alcatraz Island and to several of the World War II-era internment camps the U.S. government used for Japanese-Americans." Waterboarding is back "and other forms of torture" as a means to glean lifesaving information about looming terror attacks. And "Trump has also ordered airstrikes on the family members of known terrorists from Afghanistan to Libya."

Samuelsohn acknowledged the low likelihood of his conspiracy-filled future becoming a reality but endeavored anyway in building his despotic Trump-era America. He interviewed over a dozen members of Congress, legal experts, and former Capitol Hill administration and presidential campaign aides to produce his 2,500-word delusion disguised as journalism. Forget the facts necessary to prove a case for impeachment and pass constitutional muster or that such an undertaking would be to deliberately overturn the will of the almost 63 million Americans who elected Donald Trump. *Pish-tosh.* "The genesis of impeachment," admitted Representative Al Green (D-TX) in December 2019, "to be very candid with you, was when the president was running for office." Donald Trump committed an impeachable offense before being sworn in as president? Earlier that year, Representative Green let the mask slip again, conceding that he was "concerned that if we don't impeach the president, he will get re-elected."

The campaign to oust Trump was under way long before the elite media and Democrats seized on President Trump's now-infamous July 2019 phone call with Ukrainian president Volodymyr Zelensky. More than a week before Democrats voted in February 2020 to impeach President Trump, Paul Begala, CNN political contributor and former adviser to President Bill Clinton, admitted, reluctantly, that he discussed impeaching Trump with House Speaker Nancy Pelosi. "I had this conversation, I probably shouldn't say—a conversation with Nancy Pelosi right after the Democrats won the majority, said that too. You should impeach the president when the Republicans ask you to, and not before. It has to be bipartisan. And yet it's not," Begala said.

Democrats won 41 seats in November 2018, giving them that House majority Begala mentioned. But the truth is, Democrats and their media allies had been banging the drum of impeachment nearly every day, every month for the first 35-plus months of Trump's post-election life.

Calling for the Impeachment of President Trump

- **November 10, 2016 (two days after the election): "If he takes the risk of going to trial and he's convicted, that could be seen as an impeachable offense." —George Stephanopoulos, *Good Morning America* host and former Bill Clinton communications director**
- **March 2017: "That tweet fits the Republican definition of an impeachable offense more fully than what Bill Clinton was actually impeached for." —Lawrence O'Donnell, MSNBC host**

- **September 2018: "This tweet alone is grounds for impeachment." —Jeffrey Toobin, CNN legal analyst**

Most Americans, even those uninterested in high-stakes political enmity, watched this noxious witch hunt unfold. But it turns out, Americans had seen this movie before. I mean long before. As unique as Donald Trump's meteoric rise to the White House was, he's typical as it pertains to the political left's decadeslong ritual of impeachment politics. Democrats have tried to impeach every elected Republican president since Dwight D. Eisenhower left office in 1961. Richard Nixon, Ronald Reagan, George H. W. Bush, George W. Bush, and Donald Trump all had articles of impeachment drawn up and introduced against them by congressional Democrats. (They didn't attempt to impeach Gerald Ford, who was appointed vice president by Nixon instead of being elected.)

President Trump was acquitted by the Senate on February 5, 2020, after a two-month House inquiry, on the impeachment charges of abuse of power and obstruction of Congress. Five days later, the *Washington Post* ran a headline that pointed to the impeachment-paved road the Democrats were planning to drag America back down again: "Trump is right. We might have to impeach him again."

15.

TRUMP HAS BEEN TOUGHER ON PUTIN THAN OBAMA WAS

It's the commonest of common knowledge among America's wealthy and powerful: In the words of House Speaker Nancy Pelosi, when it comes to Trump, "all roads lead to Putin."

Left-wing dogma proposes that President Trump has gone out of his way to accommodate Russian foreign policy and enable Putin to trudge along the path to global hegemony unimpeded. The left's reasoning is that either Putin has blackmailed Trump with personal information somehow more scandalous than the content of nationally broadcast *Celebrity Apprentice* episodes, or that the two leaders simply share an ideological affinity. Putin is, the left claims, far more powerful at the tail end of President Trump's first term than President Obama's last.

Never mind Obama telling Putin puppet and then-president Dmitry Medvedev in 2012 that, after securing a second term, he would have "more flexibility" to act in Russia's benefit. Also left unmentioned are Putin's great invasions of the Obama era: the full annexation of Ukraine's Crimean peninsula in 2014 and Russia's dominance on the Syrian battlefield for most of Obama's two terms. Putin's top diplomat, Foreign Minister Sergey Lavrov, told reporters that his counterpart under Obama, John Kerry, approved of the illegal Crimean conquest.

Trump-Putin Tweets

"[Trump is a] miscreant who traded [*sic*] pathetic soul [*sic*] Putin, in exchange presidency [*sic*]."
—Cher, iconic pop diva

"This moron, puppet, coward sided with Putin over our own intelligence agencies! On a world stage!! Based on nothing more than Putin's word! Why??"
—Chris Evans, actor, said of Trump in a more measured analysis than Cher

"We all know that Vladimir Putin is holding something over Donald Trump. We do not know what it is, but we know it must be something extraordinary because no rational politician, no rational president would act this way if he weren't being blackmailed on some level." —Joe Scarborough, MSNBC host, boldly declared

Putin invaded Georgia in 2008, before Obama took office, but by the time Obama left, the Russians had carved out a rebel republic with little resistance and Mikheil Saakashvili, the president who had defied Putin and stopped a full-blown Russian invasion, had fled to Ukraine.

In the face of an increasingly belligerent Russia, Obama moved to weaken the defense of U.S. allies in the region during his first year in office. Heralded as one of the most striking differences between Obama and predecessor George W. Bush, Obama canceled a plan to build elaborate missile defense systems in Poland and the Czech Republic in September 2009. The Bush Pentagon had planned to build missile defense systems in those countries, which were so often turned into battlefields between the Germans and Russians in the twentieth century. They were nominally intended to protect Europe from long-range missiles developed by Russia's ally Iran. Obama claimed he would redirect efforts toward "stronger, swifter, and smarter" defense systems.

If intended as a goodwill gesture for Iran, it was Russia who got the message. Russian Foreign Ministry spokesman Andrei Nesterenko called it "obviously a positive sign for us." Medvedev called it a "responsible move."

While weakening the United States' allies, Obama emboldened Russia's. The $150 million the 2015 nuclear deal handed to Iran's Islamic Revolutionary government largely went into bolstering the tyranny of Russian ally Bashar al-Assad in Syria. Obama opened American corporations to enriching the communist dictatorship of Cuba, which gave Russia the confidence to write off Cuba's debt in exchange for letting Russia explore for oil and gas in Cuban waters, which border American waters.

But this chapter isn't about Obama. Even if he had not adopted policies that greatly elevated Russia's profile around the world, Trump would still be among the most frustrating American presidents modern Russia has faced. Far from trading his "pathetic soul" to Putin, Trump has thwarted the Russian forever president at every turn, from exposing Moscow's human rights violations against Christians to imposing sanctions on the economically hobbled state to weakening Putin's nefarious allies.

Under President Trump, Russian misdeeds both within the nation's borders and abroad have met with swift punishment. Every year, the Trump State Department's annual report, like that of its predecessor, has condemned Moscow for its violent repression of non-Orthodox Christians, particularly Jehovah's Witnesses, Pentecostals, Jews, and Muslims outside Chechnya, where Putin-allied strongman Ramzan Kadyrov imposes a reign of terror on his people. "Media and NGOs reported the killing of a deputy imam and a number of physical assaults based on religious identity," the State Department stated in 2017 in its report. "There were physical assaults on Jehovah's Witnesses, Pentecostals, Muslims, and Jews, as well as other attacks on individuals, which may have been based on both their ethnicity and religion." However, the Trump administration has accompanied condemnation with action, banning two Russian officials from entering the country in September 2019 for their ties to the persecution of Jehovah's Witnesses. "Russia should end its unjust campaign against the Jehovah's Witnesses and immediately release the over 200 individuals it currently has imprisoned for exercising their freedom of religion or belief," State Department spokeswoman Morgan Ortagus said at the time.

The Trump administration's focus on Christian persecution in Russia is particularly important in light of Putin's public image. Throughout his tenure at the helm of the country, Putin has attempted to portray himself as a champion of Russian Christian culture, either at home with the persecution of LGBT Russians or abroad by supporting Assad in Syria, who makes similarly false claims to be a friend of all Christians.

Trump has not taken any more favorably to Russia's actions in

Syria. In 2018, Trump responded to fresh reports of Assad once again violating international law with a chemical weapons attack on civilians by ordering airstrikes against Syrian targets. The strikes weakened a key Russian ally at a time when polls showed Russians were fatigued by Putin's insistence on having a role in the Syrian civil war.

The White House under Trump also hasn't been charitable when Russia itself, and not its proxies, uses chemical weapons. Also in 2018, Trump expanded sanctions on Russia in response to the attempted poisoning of former spy Sergei Skripal in London. More Skripal-related sanctions came down in 2019, significantly limiting Russia's access to American banks and banning loans from international financial institutions.

Trump also expelled sixty Russian government officials from the Russian embassy in Washington in response to the attack, and significantly limited Russia's reach in the United States elsewhere. Via the *Washington Post*:

> **Sixty Russians were expelled from the United States alone in retaliation for the poisoning of a former Russian spy in Britain. Twelve Russian diplomats at the United Nations in New York and 48 at the Russian Embassy in Washington face expulsion within seven days. The United States also ordered the closure of the Russian Consulate in Seattle.**

Then there was the response to Russian activity against the United States, not just violations of international law. Here lies the most damning action by the Trump administration against the claim that seems to drive much of left-wing hysteria against the president: that Putin somehow "hacked" the 2016 election to steal it on behalf of Trump. In reality, the actual allegation is that Russian disinformation agents engaged in exhaustive efforts to post confusing and poorly worded memes online meant to manipulate U.S. election results, such as a "gay Bernie Sanders" online coloring book and an image of Jesus arm-wrestling Satan to stop Hillary Clinton from winning the election. There is little evidence suggesting even a single American voter weighed these memes in the voting booth.

Incompetent as the attempts may have been, meddling in American elections is a crime and the Trump administration punished it. In 2016, the U.S. government sanctioned five entities and nineteen individuals for "malign Russian cyber activity, including their attempted interference in U.S. elections, destructive cyber-attacks, and intrusions targeting critical infrastructure," according to Treasury Secretary Steven Mnuchin. The sanctions limit Americans' ability to do business with Russian Internet companies and cut off the reach of the named entities into American media. The sanctions against Russia that have been passed under Trump are nearly too numerous to name. Diplomats, local officials responsible for repression, and even prized members of the oligarchy like Putin's son-in-law Kirill Shamalov have been affected.

Trump has not limited his Russia containment policies to sanctions—though he has imposed them on the regime more than a dozen times—he has acted to strengthen allies particularly vulnerable to Russian military actions. Trump has expanded weapons sales to both Ukraine and Georgia. He also made up for the missile defense system Poland lost and then some in 2019, signing the largest arms purchase deal in the history of Poland to sell the nation a $4.75 billion missile defense system. Talks to revamp the entire Polish military with purchases of American fighter jets occurred throughout 2019. And then there is "Fort Trump"—a proposed permanent American military base in Poland, which Warsaw has reportedly offered $2 billion to help build. Trump has so far agreed to deploy at least 1,000 more troops to the Eastern European country.

16.

BORDER CROSSINGS PLUMMETED BY 78 PERCENT FROM MARCH 2019 TO MARCH 2020

By February 2020, the Mexican military was successfully blocking thousands of Central American migrants from illegally crossing the U.S.-Mexico border. Daily apprehensions of migrants by U.S. Customs and Border Protection (CBP) agents, which had hit a high of 4,600, were down to roughly 1,300. The 21-daily average was well below 1,000. That represented a "dramatic reduction" of 78 percent, according to Mark A. Morgan, acting U.S. Customs and Border Protection commissioner. There was also a decline in apprehensions of families for a ninth consecutive month, with a 10.7 percent drop to 4,610 from the previous month. Family unit apprehensions were down 87.4 percent in January 2020 from just a year earlier.

Customs and Border Patrol data showed that between February and March 2020 there were about 33,937 attempted border crossings. There were nearly 104,000 attempted border crossings in March 2019.

The reduction in overall apprehensions was the result of a string of asylum-centric agreements and a multifaceted enforcement effort launched in the early days of the Trump administration.

The first of many moves the president would make to fortify the southwestern border was his January 2017 executive order, asking Congress to hire 5,000 additional Border Patrol officers. Lawmakers balked. By the end of 2019, Congress had authorized an increase of only about 1,200 new Border Patrol officers. The president, as noted by the Migration Policy Institute (MPI), spent many months throughout his first term in office using the wide-ranging power of the executive office to stifle the flow of Central American and Mexican migrants passing through the legal ports of entry. Once on our shores, they received myriad legal protections offered to them under a slew of international laws and domestic statutes.

In June 2017, the Trump administration announced that it would end an AmeriCorps initiative that provided lawyers to represent in immigration court the thousands of unaccompanied minors who had been apprehended at the border. Privately funded attorneys as well as law school students, like those at UNLV's law school, continued to represent these children during immigration proceedings. Two months later, the Trump White House announced that the Department of State would soon stop accepting new applications for the Central American Minors (CAM) refugee program, an Obama-era initiative that had long provided processing for refugee minors in El Salvador, Guatemala, and Honduras. By January 2018, the government had halted all interviews of minors in those countries.

In December 2017, U.S. Immigration and Customs Enforcement (ICE) ended an Obama-era order that saw the government release pregnant women from federal custody into the United States while they awaited their immigration hearings. Previous administrations had detained pregnant women, but the Obama White House issued a late-2016 policy that ordered ICE to "generally" release expectant mothers who were apprehended by Border Patrol agents. Detainees declined from 1,380 pregnant women in calendar year 2016 to 1,160 in 2017. The number spiked in 2018 to 2,098, according to a Government Accountability Office report.

In 2018, the Trump administration intensified its work site enforcement raids. "We've already increased the number of inspections in work site operations; you will see that significantly increase this next fiscal year," said then–acting ICE director Thomas Homan in October 2017. "Not only are we going to prosecute the employers that hire illegal workers, we're going to detain and remove the illegal alien workers. When we find you at a work site, we're no longer going to turn our heads. We'll go after the employer who knowingly hires an illegal alien . . . but we're always going to arrest a person who is here illegally. That is our job." Work site investigations jumped from 1,691 in fiscal year 2017 to 6,848 opened investigations in 2018. Another 6,812 such probes were initiated in 2019. ICE made 106 work site arrests in 2016. That number increased sharply in 2018 to roughly 1,600 and rose again in 2019 to 2,048. Charges against employers who hire illegal laborers are still nonexistent. And the number of employers arrested for hiring illegal aliens has declined since 2016; there were 72 in 2018 and just 40 in 2019.

President Trump has also, on several occasions, ordered the U.S. military to the southwestern border. The Department of Defense deployed 4,000 members of the National Guard to the southern border in April 2018. By March 2019, about 2,100 National Guard members remained stationed on the border. In October 2018 the president ordered the Defense Department to deploy 5,200 active-duty personnel to the U.S.-Mexico border. The decision to send thousands of armed military personnel to the border was meant to thwart the estimated 6,000 migrants from Central America heading toward the United States. "We're bringing in military police units. We're bringing in strategic airlift," said U.S. Northern Command Commander Air Force General Terrence O'Shaughnessy. "As we sit right now, we have three C-130s and a C-17 that is ready to deploy with [Customs and Border Protection] personnel wherever they need to be."

In the summer of 2019, President Trump had threatened Mexico's government with a progressive tariff—5 percent on Mexican goods, which would increase every month until they reached 25 percent—in exchange for a vote and subsequent action by Mexico to use its military might to stop the near-unchecked siege of migrant caravans pouring across the border into the United States. In June, the State Department announced a joint declaration (between Mexico and the United States) stating that "those [migrants] crossing the U.S. Southern Border to seek asylum will be rapidly returned to Mexico where they may await the adjudication of their [U.S.] asylum claims. . . . Mexico will authorize the entrance of all of those individuals for humanitarian reasons, in compliance with its international obligations, while they await the adjudication of their asylum claims." Mexico will also provide jobs, healthcare, and education to the migrants.

Dubbed the "Remain in Mexico" policy, it effectively ended the "catch-and-release" rule, which had been cooked up by the courts and Congress. Catch and release had long left border officials powerless to decide whether to allow migrants accompanied by children to legally enter the United States by claiming asylum. Instead, border officials were forced to automatically grant such migrants entry. As a result of the agreement, Mexico deployed 15,000 military and national guard troops to its northern border. "In the northern part of the country, we have deployed a total of almost 15,000 troops composed of national guard elements and military units," Mexican secretary of defense Luis Cresencio Sandoval told reporters during a briefing. Sandoval also announced the deployment of 2,000 guardsmen to Mexico's southern border. At the time, there were roughly 400,000 migrants from Central America and other countries marching through Mexico on their way to the United States.

In late March 2020, the president issued emergency health declarations to mitigate the spread of the COVID-19 coronavirus, which originated in China and had spread to every continent around the world. Closing the nation's borders to all noncitizens was a critical part of reducing the impact of the coronavirus in the United States. The Centers for Disease Control and Prevention (CDC) issued an emergency public health order that went into effect on March 21. As a result, CBP announced that it had dropped the number of detainees at its facilities from 20,000 to under 100 by expelling them from the southern border. The emergency declaration also gave the agency the power to carry out rapid expulsions of those caught illegally crossing the border. "Those who are undocumented or don't have documents or authorization are turned away," Morgan said.

17.

TRUMP WAGED ECONOMIC WAR ON ANTI-LGBT NATIONS, STARTING WITH PUTIN ALLY AND RUSSIA'S CHECHNYA REGION LEADER RAMZAN KADYROV

When Donald Trump won the presidency, many in the mainstream media marveled at the overwhelming support he garnered from Christian Evangelical voters. In 2016, 81 percent of Evangelicals voted for Trump. That number eclipsed what Mitt Romney or George W. Bush received. And both men lived much more publicly devout lives than the tabloid-playboy-turned-reality-TV-show-host.

These voters, and their high-profile advocates, expected Trump to see their vote as a mandate to advance their interests: support for religious freedom and acceptance of conservative lifestyles, after eight years of an openly progressive president Barack Obama, who disparaged religious conservatives as "bitter" before even taking the oath of office. Faith-based voters have by and large received the support they sought. The Trump administration has championed religious freedom, and raised the prickly topic of Christian perse-cution, at nearly every opportunity, welcoming Christian groups to the White House and embracing campaigns to prevent judicial over-reach from silencing the faithful.

Trump, however, has not allowed this proximity to distort his support for the rights of LGBT individuals around the world.

"The Obama administration has not only sent openly gay ambassadors into countries that are culturally opposed to homosexuality, they've used foreign aid to force nations opposed to homosexuality to change their laws to provide special protections for such behavior," Family Research Council leader Tony Perkins protested the month before Trump's inauguration. "The incoming administration needs to make clear that these liberal policies will be reversed and the 'activists' within the State Department promoting them will be ferreted out and will be replaced by conservatives who will ensure the State Department focuses on true international human rights like religious liberty which is under unprecedented assault."

Perkins demanded Trump reconsider appointing Rex Tillerson his first secretary of state.

Trump ignored Perkins's advice on this issue while simultaneously hiring him to run the United States Commission on International Religious Freedom (USCIRF). The USCIRF has played a key role in the Trump administration's campaign not just to pressure authoritarian states to protect Christian minorities, but to defend the rights of persecuted Muslims worldwide (see chapter 11).

Disregarding Perkins's harried dispatch while giving him a role in the administration that played to his strengths is perhaps one of the clearest examples of Trump's unprecedented ability to balance support for all individual rights, even when American politics pits them against each other.

Trump has supported the right of LGBT individuals to serve in the military for decades and endorsed the expansion of laws against discrimination to include gay people. He maintained record levels of support from the Evangelical community while famously waving an LGBT pride flag at one of his 2016 campaign rallies and advocating for more LGBT inclusivity within the Republican Party. As president, Trump has vocally embraced respect for the rights of LGBT people, appointed LGBT officials to some of his administration's highest positions, championed policies that impact gay communities, and allowed his officials the space to clash with homophobes when necessary.

Left-wing gay rights groups have attempted to erase these initiatives largely by warning that Trump would soon use his presidential power to crush pro-LGBT initiatives. In few realms were they louder than regarding Trump's power to appoint justices to the Supreme Court. Outraged leftist groups sounded the alarm on Justices Neil Gorsuch and Brett Kavanaugh, demanding the American people simply take their predictive powers at face value.

"Gorsuch is a conservative justice in the tradition of Justice [Antonin] Scalia. As such, he is likely to reach decisions that negatively impact many parts of the LGBT community when considering issues of race, immigration, and reproductive health," an analysis from the UCLA School of Law declared, citing an opinion Gorsuch joined "recognizing that a transgender person can state a claim for sex discrimination."

Just as with his confirmation generally, the debate on Kavanaugh's LGBT rights stances was far more unhinged. Kavanaugh, mainstream outlets breathlessly repeated, had no record of ruling on LGBT cases, which somehow proved he is a bigot.

The Media Fails to Find Kavanaugh's Anti-LGBT Sentiment

"Justice Brett Kavanaugh would represent an immediate threat to LGBT rights," the left-wing *Salon* proclaimed. "Kavanaugh is widely perceived as further to the right on LGBT rights issues than [outgoing Justice Anthony] Kennedy. And if he is seated on the high court, there is a strong chance that Kavanaugh will become part of a majority that will vote to start rolling back LGBT rights within the next year."

"LGBT Advocates Fear Kavanaugh's Votes on Gay-Rights Issues," an Associated Press headline blared, on an article in which a cited expert said, "I don't think he is going to be a knee-jerk judge in any direction, and I don't think he is anti-LGBT."

The *Daily Beast*, failing to find any evidence that Kavanaugh hates gay people, published the resigned headline, "Where Does Brett Kavanaugh Stand on LGBT Rights? It's a Mystery."

The Supreme Court is currently considering, to be decided in 2020, a series of cases in which plaintiffs argue that civil rights protections extend to people on the basis of their sexual identity. Doomsday predictions of homophobic declarations from Kavanaugh or Gorsuch have failed to materialize. Kavanaugh has angered the left by saying nothing indicative of his thinking on the case in either direction. Gorsuch, meanwhile, has "emerged as a possible LGBT ally," according to gay newspaper the *Washington Blade*.

"Gorsuch, a Trump-appointed justice who considers himself a textualist, asked many questions suggesting he's at least considering the idea that anti-LGBT discrimination is a form of sex discrimination, thus prohibited under Title VII of the Civil Rights Act of 1964," the *Blade* reported during arguments in October 2019. "If LGBT rights supporters eke out a victory from the Supreme Court, they may well have Gorsuch to thank on the divided court for taking them over the finish line."

As LGBT individuals face significantly more bigotry abroad than in the United States—69 countries, mostly in the Muslim world, identify homosexual activity as a crime in their legal codes— Trump has had to do some heavy lifting on gay rights abroad. After months of outrage from the left accusing Trump of being too close to Vladimir Putin, one of the first targets of Trump's gay rights agenda was, ironically, Russia.

In December 2017, the Trump administration used the Global Magnitsky Act, which allows the executive branch to sanction individuals for human rights abuses, to sanction Ramzan Kadyrov, the brutal leader of Russia's Chechnya region. A close friend of Putin's, Kadyrov is one of the world's most outspoken bigots against LGBT people and believed to be responsible for waging "purges" in which Chechen families are encouraged to give up relatives suspected of being gay; authorities disappear the government's own suspects. When confronted with evidence of the atrocities he has ordered his government to commit against suspected gay people, Kadyrov has denied their existence entirely. "We don't have those kinds of people here. We don't have any gays. If there are any, take them to Canada," Kadyrov said in a 2017 interview.

Trump's administration was the first to sanction Kadyrov and condemn him publicly for these abuses in a formal manner. The sanctions froze any assets Kadyrov had in the United States and banned him from entering the country.

Tillerson may be gone, but his successor, Mike Pompeo, has retained his emphasis on defending human rights, and LGBT rights specifically, on the world stage.

In 2019, the State Department took the policies behind the sanctions on Kadyrov global. Trump announced in February of that year a global initiative to pressure the nations of the world still criminalizing the existence of gay people to change their laws, spearheaded by the most prominent openly gay official in the Trump administration and arguably his most powerful envoy, Richard Grenell, ambassador to Germany. Grenell took a commanding role in implementing some of the Trump administration's most important foreign policy initiatives, from demanding European NATO countries pay more to urging Germany and others in Western Europe to stop enriching the Islamic regime in Iran, which regularly executes individuals suspected of being gay.

"This is a bipartisan push. People understand—religious people, individuals who may not always be in the LGBTI fight—they understand that criminalizing homosexuality is absolutely wrong," Grenell told NBC News about the initiative. "It is unbelievable to believe that in today's world a 32-year-old man in Iran can be hanged simply for being gay. That's unacceptable."

At the United Nations, Grenell listed, one by one, the countries that still criminalize the existence of gay people, refusing to exclude countries that have sought favorable relations with the Trump administration, like Saudi Arabia and Iraq.

As has come to be expected from the Trump administration, Christian groups were represented at the launch of the campaign.

"We are building a broad alliance around an area of profound agreement rather than on the contentious edges on the broader discussions," USCIRF commissioner and Evangelical community leader Johnnie Moore told the *Christian Post* after attending the meeting to launch the initiative. "Everyone can agree that no one in the world should be imprisoned, tortured or executed for homosexuality. Full stop. The evangelical community and the religious freedom community are in total agreement on this point and we are proud to work together with the LGBT community to eradicate these unjust laws."

The summer after the initiative launched at the United Nations was the first in which a Republican president wished the country a happy LGBT Pride Month in June—and the effects of the administration's efforts began to emerge. Botswana moved to decriminalize gay sex, a move seen favorably by the Trump administration. In Zambia, the State Department had no such luck, but supported then-Ambassador Daniel Foote in using less-than-diplomatic language to condemn the brutality of imprisoning people for their sexual identity. Foote notably condemned homophobes for distorting the message of Christianity in a press statement in December. "Discriminatory and homophobic laws, under the false flags of Christianity and culture, continue to kill innocent Zambians, many of whom were born with [HIV]," he wrote on the eve of World AIDS Day. "Your citizens are terrified of being outed as HIV-positive, because of the inaccurate and archaic associations between HIV and homosexuality.

"My job as U.S. Ambassador is to promote the interests, values, and ideals of the United States," Foote added. "Zambia is one of the largest per-capita recipients of U.S. assistance in the world, at $500 million each year. In these countries where we contribute resources, this includes partnering in areas of mutual interest, and holding the recipient government accountable for its responsibilities under this partnership.

"Lamentably, I will be unable to attend tomorrow's AIDS Day events because of threats made against me, via various media, over my comments on the harsh sentencing of homosexuals," Foote noted, condemning the "venom" he received for promoting the Trump initiative on decriminalizing LGBT people.

Zambia declared Foote, a Trump appointee, persona non grata by default, proclaiming that it was "no longer tenable" for him to remain in the country. A spokesperson for the State Department said the administration was "dismayed" and that threats against Foote would not change America's policies.

Much of the world remains violently unwelcoming to LGBT people, and the Trump administration will have its work cut out for it for years to come. But the president has put the world on notice: His administration will not tolerate human rights abuses against any targeted group for any reason. Perhaps most uniquely, it has done so while maintaining the support of conservative groups that have often seen religious freedom and gay rights as a zero-sum game. This was achieved by giving representation to conservative groups on the front lines of the war on LGBT hate.

18.

POLITICALLY MOTIVATED ARRESTS OF CUBANS PLUMMETED BY THOUSANDS IN 2019

Of all the ways that the left and the elite media have identified Trump as a bigot—a racist, a sexist, somehow both an anti-Semite and too pro-Israel—most critics put his alleged hatred for America's Hispanic community at the top of the list of smears. The most commonly cited Trump quote as a "confession" of his distaste for Latin Americans is an observation he made on the campaign trail in 2015 about how, after two Obama terms featuring an unprecedented rise in the power of drug cartels on the border, "the U.S. has become a dumping ground for everybody else's problems.

"When Mexico sends its people, they're not sending their best. They're not sending you . . . They're sending people that have lots of problems, and they're bringing those problems with us. They're bringing drugs. They're bringing crime. They're rapists. And some, I assume, are good people," Trump said.

Trump concluded by making the point that many of these alleged criminals are not Mexican, but "we don't know, because we have no protection and we have no competence."

The left and its allies and enablers in the media proceeded to interpret the speech, which explicitly noted both that not all illegal immigrants are criminals and not all criminals are Mexican, as indisputable proof that Trump thought all Mexicans were "rapists."

"Donald Trump is a bigot and a racist," concluded noted Latino connoisseur Dana Milbank.

In 2019, the leftist dogma that Trump hated Hispanics and wanted them dead somehow became even more alarmist. "Is It Still Safe to Be a Latino in Donald Trump's United States?" an actual *Daily Beast* headline asked after the 2019 El Paso shooting by a white supremacist (whose ideology had no visible ties to the Trump administration and whose actions Trump, of course, repudiated). Raúl Reyes, a columnist for *USA Today*, declared that Trump had made it "open season" on Latin Americans in the country.

His approval rating among Hispanic Americans has largely hovered around 30 percent in his first term.

The Hispanic community is a piecemeal invention, however, a tapestry of nationalities, religions, races, and even languages that statisticians use as an organizational tool. And within that tapestry there is a major exception in attitudes toward President Trump: Cuban Americans.

In 2016, Trump made history by securing the first-ever presidential endorsement from the survivors of Brigade 2506, the veterans of John F. Kennedy's betrayal at the Bay of Pigs. There is a case to be made that Cubans won Trump Florida, a key electoral college state, and quite possibly the presidency. Florida Cubans were twice as likely to vote for Trump as other Latinos. As late as July 2019, Cuban Americans were still singing President Trump's praises. An NPR correspondent interviewed first- and second-generation Cuban immigrants living in Miami to see what their response was to President Trump telling four Democratic congresswomen to "go back and help fix the totally broken and crime-infested places from which they came."

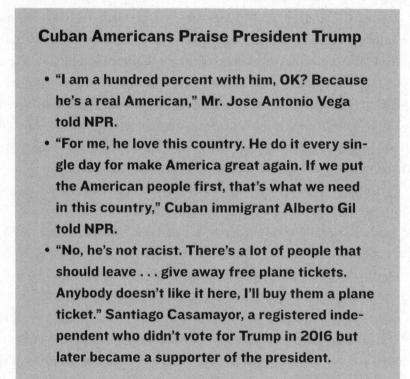

Cuban Americans Praise President Trump

- "I am a hundred percent with him, OK? Because he's a real American," Mr. Jose Antonio Vega told NPR.
- "For me, he love this country. He do it every single day for make America great again. If we put the American people first, that's what we need in this country," Cuban immigrant Alberto Gil told NPR.
- "No, he's not racist. There's a lot of people that should leave . . . give away free plane tickets. Anybody doesn't like it here, I'll buy them a plane ticket." Santiago Casamayor, a registered independent who didn't vote for Trump in 2016 but later became a supporter of the president.

To understand this political phenomenon, we must look back to another iconic Trump quote on Latin American issues, one that seems to have conveniently gotten lost on its way to mainstream media headlines. In 1999, and again in 2000 in his book *The America We Deserve*, Trump made a promise to America's Cuban exile community, one that he kept, and then some, when entering the White House.

"Several large European investment groups have asked me to take the 'Trump Magic' to Cuba. They have 'begged' me to form partnerships to build casino-hotels in Havana," Trump wrote in the *Miami Herald* in 1999. "With the influx of foreign tourists, we would make a fortune, they promise, and they are no doubt right. . . . But rushing to join those who would do business in Cuba would do more than that. It would place me directly at odds with the longstanding U.S. policy of isolating Fidel Castro. I had a choice to make: huge profits or human rights. For me, it was a no-brainer," Trump concluded.

He went on to note the tired arguments for lifting the embargo— the economically libertarian and near-religious belief that "the market" would free Cuba, that tossing money at the murderous regime would catalyze democracy. If Cubans see how wealthy they could be under capitalism, the argument goes, they would become capitalist.

"Each of those arguments is bogus," Trump wrote. "Almost every dollar would go to prop up his police-state. Why? Because foreign investors cannot legally do business with private Cuban citizens. They can go into business only with the Castro government." He continued:

If I formed a joint venture with European partners, I would make millions of dollars. But I'd rather lose those millions than lose my self-respect. I would rather take

a financial hit than become a financial backer of one of the world's most-brutal dictators, a man who was once willing to aid in the destruction of my country. To me the embargo question is no question at all. Of course, we should keep the embargo in place. We should keep it until Castro is gone.

A year later, in his book, Trump went one step further, urging any nation to which Fidel Castro traveled to arrest him and try him in the United States on terrorism charges. "Fidel is a criminal," Trump wrote. "Let's treat him like one."

The Cuban American community is a tiny sliver of the American populace, so suffice it to say that Trump's thoughts on Fidel Castro were not exactly at the top of the list of issues most voters considered in 2016.

The Cuban exile community, however, has not forgotten his words, in part because he has kept to his promise as president. But it is almost impossible to forget a multibillionaire businessman asserting himself in the name of the Cuban people so vocally because it is almost entirely unheard of. And no time since the Cold War began has made this so vividly and cruelly true than the Obama era.

In a dramatic contrast to Trump's hard-line pro-embargo stance, Obama announced a policy in 2014 of slowly repealing the embargo, using an expansionist interpretation of executive power to repeal State Department limits on tourism there. Obama brokered deals with Havana to allow giant corporations like airlines and cruise lines to go into business with the regime (it remains illegal for Cuban people to do business outside the Communist Party). Obama expanded "people to people" travel, an exception to the embargo that allowed tourism if you just didn't call it "tourism." He reopened the U.S. embassy in Havana and allowed the Cubans to send their own diplomats to Washington, free to engage in the kind of espionage operations that have killed U.S. citizens.

Speaking of killing U.S. citizens, President Obama also released the "Cuban Five," a deadly communist spy network responsible for the deaths of Carlos Costa, Armando Alejandre, Mario de la Peña, and Pablo Morales. Obama even shipped the Cuban government one of the Cuban Five's sperm so that he could have a baby waiting for him when he got back.

Obama himself took advantage of non-tourism tourism to Cuba in 2016, enjoying a baseball game with Raúl Castro and taking photos in front of an image of mass murderer Ernesto "Che" Guevara. The Castro regime tallied near-record numbers of politically motivated, violent arrests during President Obama's visit in March of that year, "collateral damage," as one dissident put it.

Trump may think a burrito bowl is "Hispanic" food, but Cubans are pretty sure they will never catch him doing the wave with Raúl Castro.

Taking office in 2017, President Trump completely changed the tenor of relations with Havana. His national security strategy vowed to "isolate governments that refuse to act as responsible partners in advancing hemispheric peace and prosperity," identifying Cuba and Venezuela by name. Sanctions on Cuba and Venezuela for domestic human rights abuses have hit nearly every powerful member of the Castro regime, including Raúl Castro himself.

Trump has significantly reduced the legal ways to spend money in Cuba's hotel system, which is almost entirely owned by the Cuban military. "People to people" travel is no longer legal, shutting down the pipeline of celebrity-and-classic-car photo shoots that will now be remembered as an anomaly of the Obama era. Sorry, Tim McGraw and Richard Branson, you were late.

Trump also banned the cruise-ship travel that Obama legalized, which funneled billions to the Castro regime and initially violated the Civil Rights Act. Cuba wanted to ban Americans of ethnic Cuban descent from the ships and Carnival Cruises was happy to oblige before it got sued.

In late 2019, Trump closed a loophole in federal appropriations that allowed for the use of taxpayers' dollars for "educational and cultural exchange" with Cuba, one with high risk of abuse in the same manner that the "people to people" exception was.

In the sports world, Trump intervened to prevent Major League Baseball (MLB) from signing a deal with the Castro regime that would have endangered Cuban athletes seeking to defect to a free country. Cuba is famously flush with baseball talent, and many young players through the years have defected abroad and come to America, signing multimillion-dollar deals with U.S. baseball teams. The deal with Havana would have made that impossible, giving young Cubans basically no good reason to try to make it in the baseball world.

In politics, Trump has made it loud and clear that his administration sides with pro-democracy dissidents, not with the regime. And while Trump continues to receive scorn for allegedly seeking to keep Latin Americans out of the country, the Trump administration has invited dissidents to attend events on Cuba held in the United States.

Trump has consistently put them in the spotlight, inviting people like José Daniel Ferrer—leader of the Patriotic Union of Cuba, the largest dissident group on the island—and Berta Soler, the head of the Catholic Ladies in White dissident group, to events focusing on Cuba. Rather than elevate their killers, Trump invited the relatives of the Brothers to the Rescue members the Cuban regime killed to a key Cuba policy speech in 2017. Most recently, Washington offered a humanitarian visa to Xiomara Cruz in January 2020, a Ladies in White member in a delicate state of health who believed the Castro regime deliberately poisoned her or infected her with a virus.

The result of this policy has been a Cuba with a dramatically weakened ability to oppress its people. Statistics for 2019 on politically motivated arrests show a nosedive in the number from the Obama era, though the issue of torturing political prisoners remains a problem. The Cuban regime has increasingly attempted to turn to China for money—but China, cornered by Trump's trade strategy, is not interested. The regime remains, but it is on the defensive again, something for which all Cuban Americans should be thankful.

19.

TRUMP HAS BEEN ON A GLOBAL CAMPAIGN TO BRING HOME AMERICANS HELD HOSTAGE

"I don't agree with all the political shit that he does at all, but I'm just thankful for everybody that supported me in there. . . . Regardless of the political shit, I kept it cordial and very respectful 'cause I was thankful." It was probably the best thank-you Trump could expect from a guy who has rapped "the president is an asshole" in multiple songs. The New York rapper A$AP Rocky likely never expected to need Trump's help in any situation but, on a summer night out in Stockholm in 2019, he and his entourage found themselves in the middle of a violent scuffle that ended in his arrest. His attorneys argued that two men had followed the group and actively antagonized them before attacking them and cited ample video evidence they claimed absolved their client.

As President Trump put it on his Twitter account, "I watched the tapes of A$AP Rocky, and he was being followed and harassed by troublemakers. Treat Americans fairly!"

Trump personally accused Swedish prime minister Stefan Löfven of having "let our African American Community [*sic*] down in the

United States," only lightly insinuating that the prime minister was racist. He then demanded the Swedish government focus on its "real crime problem," likely a reference to a wave of rapes and sexual assaults in the nation's biggest cities mostly committed by migrants.

Trump had also told Prime Minister Löfven that he could personally guarantee A$AP Rocky was not a flight risk if granted bail, thus morphing the situation from a police investigation into a diplomatic negotiation, with the full force of the White House behind it. The Trump team reportedly negotiated behind the scenes in addition to Trump's Twitter barrages and, ultimately, secured the rapper's release in August. Perhaps in an attempt to prove Trump was right that he was no flight risk, A$AP Rocky returned to Sweden to perform four months later.

The A$AP Rocky international crisis of 2019 has already gone down in history as one of the most unexpected collaborations of the Trump White House. Trump publicly demanding freedom for the imprisoned rapper raised eyebrows because, in part, it shattered the image that the mainstream press had so diligently worked to create of Trump as thin-skinned and petty, never willing to overlook insults in the name of the greater good. It is also notable because it highlights one of the most successful, subtle policy initiatives of the Trump era: using every possible avenue of power—including the presidential bully pulpit—to secure the freedom of Americans imprisoned abroad, without paying terrorists or rogue regimes for their freedom.

In Trump's own words, his administration is "38–0" on negotiating for the secure release of Americans in foreign prisons. The sheer diversity of situations, backgrounds, and individuals on that list is breathtaking—rappers, yes, but also professors, pastors, business leaders, humanitarians, basketball players, and kids on vacation. Trump has threatened to destroy, and began the process of destroying, the economies of entire nations to bring these Americans home.

Perhaps the most iconic cluster of cases that the Trump administration resolved are the Americans imprisoned in North Korea. At the time of this writing, there are none, but after eight years of "strategic patience" under Barack Obama, Pyongyang felt comfortable enough to take two hostages: Otto Warmbier, a young college student accused of defacing a communist propaganda poster while on vacation in the capital, and Kim Dong Chul, a Korean American accused of espionage and suspected of being a Christian. Christianity, once so thriving in Pyongyang that the city earned the nickname "Jerusalem of the East," is a high crime in communist North Korea. Even suspicions of believing in Jesus can land a North Korean in prison.

Two others—Kim Hak Song, arrested for sending an email requesting prayers for North Korea, and Tony Kim, arrested for unspecified "hostile acts"—were arrested in 2017, bargaining chips with which to threaten a newly minted president. Trump immediately got to work on talks with North Korea, vowing a new approach of action, not "patience," and speaking plainly to the regime. He would chat with and even meet dictator Kim Jong-un—an unprecedented act—but Trump would also tighten the screws on U.S. and international sanctions on the regime, starving Kim and crushing his ability to behave recklessly.

Otto Warmbier was the first out of the gate. His grim tale, by now, is well known. He returned to his native Ohio in the summer of 2017, now twenty-two, in a coma, never to wake up again. North

Korea claimed he contracted "botulism" while in prison in a freak incident, but his body showed signs of severe abuse. He died at home, tragically, but with his parents, for which they were grateful and outraged that the prior administration did not act to resolve the matter more quickly.

> When Otto was first taken, we were advised by the past administration to take a low profile while they worked to obtain his release. We did so without result. Earlier this year, Cindy and I decided the time for strategic patience was over. . . . It is my understanding that [Special Representative for North Korea Policy Joseph Y. Yun] and his team, at the direction of the president, aggressively pursued resolution of the situation.
>
> —Fred Warmbier, Otto's father, in 2017

Otto's story may be over, but Trump has maintained contact with the Warmbiers, hosting them for dinner in September 2019, over two years after their son's return and subsequent death.

Trump would have better luck with the three other hostages.

Kim Dong Chul, Kim Hak Song, and Tony Kim all survived their ordeals in relative health and all returned home in May 2018, a month before Trump would meet Kim Jong-un in person. What's more, when North Korea had the opportunity to take another American hostage—Bruce Byron Lowrance, who reportedly entered the country via China—Pyongyang simply deported him, knowing they

would get no ransom. Trump's diplomats at the United Nations imposed unprecedentedly strict sanctions on North Korea following
its 2017 nuclear bomb test, and the administration has not relented,
creating embarrassing moments for Democrats like Joe Biden, who
claimed on a debate stage in 2020 that Trump had "weakened" sanctions on the very day the Treasury had imposed a new round of them.

Some argued that Trump traded a handshake with Kim for
those three lives, but that certainly wasn't true in the case of Pastor Andrew Brunson's jailer. Brunson was arrested in 2016, in the
aftermath of the chaotic failed coup against President Recep Tayyip
Erdoğan of Turkey. While the coup plotters themselves released a
statement declaring themselves secularist military men, Erdoğan
wove an improbable conspiracy theory that Islamic cleric Fethullah Gülen, a Pennsylvania resident, had conspired with Kurdish
Marxist forces to take him down and demanded Gülen's extradition.
He repeatedly failed to present evidence for his claims in multiple
meetings with President Trump, and American diplomats regularly
denied that their Turkish counterparts had produced a coherent
argument for Gülen's extradition.

The result was a wave of government position purges, mass
arrests, media outlet closures, and severe human rights violations
against anyone remotely suspected of having ties to Gülen or the
Kurdistan Workers Party (PKK), a U.S.-designated Marxist terrorist group.

Brunson, a Christian who had lived in Turkey for over a decade
when the coup occurred, was crushed under this torrent of oppres-
sion. Turkish prosecutors accused him of being both a Gülenist and
a PKK member—in other words, a devout Muslim and a Marxist
atheist—in a litany of charges that also included illegal "Chris-

tianization." They presented no evidence as to how Brunson could maintain three religious belief systems simultaneously or, even if he somehow did, how he had acted against the Turkish president in any way. The randomness of the charges and the frequency with which prosecutors amended them made the job of Brunson's defense team impossible.

It took about a year for Erdoğan to show his cards.

"We have given you all the documents necessary [for the extradition of Gülen]. But they say, 'give us the pastor,'" Erdoğan said in September 2017. "You have another pastor in your hands. Give us that pastor and we will do what we can in the judiciary to give you this one."

The Trump White House attempted diplomatic avenues of negotiation for months to no avail. American authorities would visit Brunson in prison to ensure his safety, find him increasingly sick and frail, and come back with nothing but bad news.

By the next summer, Trump had grown tired of friendly talks.

"To President Erdoğan and the Turkish government, I have a message on behalf of the United States of America: Release Pastor Andrew Brunson now or be prepared to face the consequences," Trump demanded in a message delivered by Mike Pence. "If Turkey does not take immediate action to free this innocent man of faith and send him home to America, the United States will impose significant sanctions on Turkey until Pastor Andrew Brunson is free."

Trump then enacted personalized sanctions on the Turkish judiciary officials responsible for the Brunson case and doubled tariffs on steel and aluminum, sinking the Turkish economy and sending Erdoğan's government into a panic.

"This reckless escalation needs to stop. . . . For everyone's sake, we should address our disagreements with diplomacy, rather than threats and provocation," Erdoğan's top diplomat, Mevlüt Çavuşoğlu, pleaded.

Erdoğan called the sanctions akin to "a direct strike . . . on our call to prayer," essentially branding them a war on all of Islam.

Pence's warning was issued in July. By October, Brunson was released. Fethullah Gülen still lives in Pennsylvania.

The list of similar cases of Trump securing the freedom of wrongfully imprisoned Americans is long and fascinating. Trump personally convinced Chinese dictator Xi Jinping to free three American college basketball players: LiAngelo Ball, Cody Riley, and Jalen Hill. His diplomats similarly negotiated the release—China called it a deportation to save face—of Houston businesswoman Sandy Pham-Gillis from that country.

In the face of sanctions not only on its bloodthirsty government but that of its colonizer state, Cuba, the socialist regime in Venezuela liberated Utah native Joshua Holt and his wife, Thamara Caleño, after framing them for stockpiling weapons and attempting unsuccessfully to demand a U.S. ransom in the form of sanctions relief.

From Egypt Trump secured the release of aid worker Aya Hijazi, imprisoned on shoddy evidence of "child abuse."

Trump's negotiation team has had significant success with non-state actors, as well. In 2017, the Taliban agreed to release American Caitlan Coleman, Canadian Joshua Boyle, and their children, some of whom were born while the couple were imprisoned. In March 2019, Trump welcomed home Danny Burch, an oil engineer released from the captivity of a gang in Yemen.

Most recently, in December 2019, Trump's sanctions on rogue

regimes yielded results in obstinate Iran, which agreed to release Princeton graduate student Xiyue Wang. Wang's case is perhaps the most notable to contrast with the strategy of the Obama administration, whose American hostage policy was largely, in one form or another, to pay up. In Wang's case, the United States did not alleviate the expansive sanctions that Trump placed on the regime in an attempt to limit its aggressive colonization attempts in Iraq, Syria, Lebanon, and elsewhere. Tehran also received no money for the prisoner, shutting down critics like former New Mexico governor Bill Richardson, who insisted a year before Wang's release that sanctions would destroy any chance of Iran releasing American hostages.

President Trump did give something up in exchange for one American: Masoud Soleimani, a stem cell researcher imprisoned on charges of trying to smuggle prohibited biological materials into Iran. It was a concession that Iran was happy with, but not one that made Tehran any more significantly a threat. Soleimani is not a nuclear physicist or bomb-maker and went home empty-handed. Back in Iran, Soleimani is not an espionage risk to Washington. The same cannot be said of the five Taliban officials President Obama released in exchange for Bowe Bergdahl, a military officer who later pleaded guilty to desertion after his release from Taliban captivity.

Mohammad Fazl, Mohammed Nabi, Abdul Haq Wasiq, Mullah Norullah Nori, and Khairullah Khairkhwa were all senior jihadist leaders in the terrorist organization when imprisoned in Guantánamo Bay. During their captivity, none showed signs of giving up their fight; intelligence experts contended that they would almost certainly return to terrorist activity as soon as they were out. What's more, subsequent reports revealed that a prisoner swap freeing them was not the only option on the table to retrieve Berg-dahl, but Obama freed them, anyway.

Some would contend it makes more sense to compare apples to apples, or Iran negotiations to Iran negotiations. While Tehran didn't get a dime for Xiyue Wang, the Obama administration openly admitted to handing over $400 million in exchange for *Washington Post* journalist Jason Rezaian, former marine Amir Hekmati, Christian pastor Saeed Abedini, and U.S. citizen Nosratollah Khosravi-Roodsari. President Obama insisted to reporters that the pallets of cash flowing into Iran as the Americans headed back home was "not a ransom," but State Department spokesman John Kirby revealed the truth with a bizarre parsing of words: officials had not given the money in exchange for the prisoners, they had just kept the money until the prisoners were released, then handed it over. "We deliberately leveraged that moment to finalize these outstanding issues nearly simultaneously," Kirby said. "With concerns that Iran may renege on the prisoner release, given unnecessary delays regarding persons in Iran who could not be located as well as, to be quite honest, mutual mistrust between Iran and the United States, we of course sought to retain maximum leverage until after American citizens were released."

While most of the examples of unsung successes in this book have been either wrongly maligned or completely ignored, Trump's record on releasing American political prisoners won praise from at least one unexpected corner of the Internet.

"Beyond the Warmbier case, the Trump administration seems to have made freeing US hostages held abroad more of a priority, and it has unquestionably had more success than the Obama administration," Alex Ward wrote following the North Korean prisoner release in 2018 at the left-wing media outlet *Vox*, contrasting Trump's legacy with Obama's using the latter's own words:

> **In 2015—six years into his presidency—then-President Obama admitted his administration had at times failed families of hostages. "It is true that there have been times where our government, regardless of good intentions, has let them down," Obama said. "I promised them that we can do better."**
>
> **Trump, it seems, is following through on that promise—to the joy of the hostages and their families.**

President Trump's secretary of state Mike Pompeo has made abundantly clear what he thinks of this legacy and how he hopes Trump's will eclipse it. "We took a very different approach. We didn't send pallets of cash . . . to the Iranians. We didn't pay for hostages," Pompeo told Fox News after the Xiyue Wang prisoner swap. In an earlier interview, he attributed the refusal to yield to rogue state pressure to Trump personally. "I think our success to date in this administration, now two years on, of getting these people back without putting a bunch of . . . cash on a pallet, by simply using American diplomacy and power to get these individuals returned home, I think our success to date is a direct function of the president's attention to these issues," Pompeo told Hugh Hewitt in a 2019 radio interview.

20.

THE TRUMP DOJ HAS OPENED MORE THAN 1,000 CASES AGAINST THE WORLD'S TOP INTELLECTUAL PROPERTY THIEVES AS AMERICA LOSES TRILLIONS TO CHINESE THEFT

We've all done it. Your blender breaks, you need an electric razor, your kid really wants a pricey Pokémon toy for his birthday. You sit down for an online shopping session and take a look at your options on Amazon. You scroll through all the tried-and-true brands that you know will last forever, but your brow furrows at the price. You sort by "price: low to high." The reshuffling reveals the ultimate temptation: basically the same product—at least that's how it looks from the pictures—at an absurdly low price, or a seemingly much more advanced product for about the same price as the simpler one you thought of getting. You meant to get an Oster blender, but you end up buying the one from AICOOK. The Phillips Norelco razor looked great, but the Ceenwes one was so much cheaper. Who knows who made this stuffed Pikachu? It came from the Wish app.

The Chinese market has made this possible. Most of those brands you've never heard of are based across the Pacific and make their goods domestically, through the use of near-slave labor in places like the southern Guangdong rust belt or actual slave labor in mostly Muslim western Xinjiang. No country has been able to compete with the output of China's factories for the same price. What those Chinese factories make, however, China has largely failed to innovate fair and square. Fueling China's manufacturing hubs is a prodigious intellectual property (IP) theft operation, one that preys mostly on American businesses for product features, fictional character branding, and overall design. While cheap, poorly made products are most often the means through which Chinese intellectual property theft crosses into the life of an average American. The theft of U.S. ideas has seeped into nearly every aspect of how our country functions.

China steals billions in information, whether it's to illegally manufacture products using trademarks that belong to U.S. companies—character branding, for example—or to manufacture complex products like cars and computers. It steals instructions for how to develop American software, American chemicals, American drugs. Chinese academics have infiltrated American universities and stolen the results of sensitive experiments and studies. Perhaps most alarmingly, Chinese agents have stolen the secrets behind advanced American military weapons and technology.

China steals in many ways: Hackers break into corporate computer networks and extract information; Chinese workers at

American companies or students at American universities take trade secrets home when they return to China; the Chinese government itself steals through mandatory "security" intrusions into foreign companies' computer systems.

On college campuses, China doesn't even try to hide it. The Chinese government launched something it calls the Thousand Talents program to flood American universities with Chinese scholars. Those scholars then steal American research and bring it home. We know because the Chinese don't deny it. Responding to American universities warning professors to protect their research in the face of potential theft of research, the *Global Times*, a Chinese government propaganda newspaper, declared, "Science belongs to all human beings."

> Some elites in the U.S. believe that China has stolen U.S. experience for its own modernization, infringing so-called US intellectual property rights. Washington is extremely puffed up with pride politically and culturally. It is also severely misunderstanding the history of human development.
> —Chinese propaganda outlet the *Global Times*

The result of this mass state-sponsored plundering? Hundreds of billions in losses to American companies—money they could have made by selling their products, but lost because a Chinese company made the same product at a much lower price. The modest estimates of the amount lost to China in intellectual property theft annually range between $150 and $240 billion a year; some studies have found as much as $600 billion a year has evaded American companies through Chinese theft.

A 2019 survey of the North American companies on the CNBC Global CFO Council found that one in five companies are aware of Chinese theft of their intellectual property. As the collective council manages nearly $5 trillion in market value, a potential $1 trillion in North American company value could be affected, much of it American.

Small companies have also fallen victim, often at a higher cost than larger, more profitable businesses.

> On multiple occasions, I've come across images of wire and sheet metal baskets on Chinese and Indian competitors' websites. They don't just look like our baskets. They *are* our baskets, being portrayed as the fruit of someone else's engineering.
> —Drew Greenblatt, president of the American company Marlin Steel, in a 2013 editorial

It's not just music, movies, and news media. This crime hits American manufacturing especially hard. Although people most identify the sector with the household-name giants that made America the best manufacturer in the world, most manufacturers are small to midsize shops that can't weather the wholesale rip-off of their intellectual property. Moreover, the thievery undercuts the very technological advantage that American businesses like mine, news media, have against foreign competition.

Before President Trump entered the White House, Washington's approach to the problem was largely to hope it goes away. The threat was treated as being somehow separate from the actions of the Chinese state. President Barack Obama implemented an approach that began first with mild exposure—two Chinese hackers indicted here, three People's Liberation Army soldiers facing prosecution there—then unsubstantiated threats of tariffs or other economic punishment. Obama succeeded in getting Chinese dictator Xi Jinping to promise to cut it out in 2015, a promise almost entirely based on the honor system—and Xi completely failed to live up to it.

The Obama administration had good reason to believe that Chinese intellectual property theft was a major drain on the American economy. Mandiant, a U.S. cybersecurity firm, warned in 2013 that People's Liberation Army—the Chinese government itself—had set up an online unit to spy on American companies and steal their information. This warning ruled out the possibility that rogue soldiers were doing the work.

President Obama responded with a campaign to indict small numbers of Chinese offenders, a warning shot across the bow to Beijing. In 2012, Obama's Justice Department indicted two DuPont employees and charged a Chinese company with stealing the instructions to make a white pigment and sending the IP to the Chinese government. A year later, prosecutors charged executives of China's largest turbine company with stealing trade secrets via a conspirator at an American company. In a May 2014 case, prosecutors indicted five Chinese soldiers on "economic espionage charges."

The pinpricks and threats of potential sanctions brought Xi Jinping to the negotiating table. In 2015, Obama and Xi announced an agreement in which China would simply promise not to steal any more American trade secrets. In exchange, Obama promised that American companies would also stop stealing trade secrets, even though there was no evidence that this was happening on any significant scale.

"I raised, once again, our very serious concerns about growing cyberthreats to American companies and American citizens. I indicated that it has to stop," Obama said after meeting with Xi. "The United States government does not engage in cyber economic espionage for commercial gain, and today I can announce that our two countries have reached a common understanding on a way forward."

A year later, NBC News bizarrely declared victory on Obama's behalf, claiming that Chinese hacking of American companies had declined and warning that Russia, not China, was the real threat. "In a rare bit of good cyber security news, Chinese hacking thefts of American corporate secrets have plummeted in the 13 months since China signed an agreement with the Obama administration to curb economic espionage, U.S. officials and outside experts say," NBC claimed in 2016. To no one's surprise, subsequent studies found that the Chinese government had violated the pact—often.

In contrast, President Trump has launched a wave of federal investigations into China's hacking—about 1,000 open cases, according to FBI Director Christopher Wray. These cases have targeted not just low-level suspected hackers or individual employees stealing trade secrets at American companies, but also some of the most powerful people in Chinese business. For example, the indictment related to telecom company Huawei's IP theft implicated the company's CFO, Meng Wanzhou, who is also the daughter of Huawei's founder. (The details of that case will be covered below.)

President Trump kept the strategy of prosecuting suspected intellectual property thieves alive. Among those cases was the 2018 indictment of Hongjin Tan, a battery expert accused of downloading confidential files from his U.S. employer to send back to the Chinese government. In another case, in 2019, Jizhong Chen was arrested for stealing intellectual property tied to Apple's upcoming self-driving car project. Unlike in the Obama era, however, there are hundreds of cases like these, and a number involve some of the most powerful people and companies in China.

"There is no country that poses a more severe counterintelligence threat to this country right now than China," FBI Director Wray said in July 2019. "It is a threat that's deep and diverse and wide and vexing. It affects basically every industry in this country." Eight months later, in February 2020, the number of open cases has remained the same, indicating that even as cases close or move through the legal system, the FBI adds new ones.

Huawei is one of China's largest companies and is involved in economic activity around the world. It landed on the FBI's list of open IP cases in 2020, facing charges of stealing "trade secret information and copyrighted works, such as source code and user manuals for internet routers, antenna technology and robot testing technology." The indictment accused Huawei of working to steal American innovation for "decades."

Trump has also addressed potential intellectual property theft through embedded Chinese agents in addition to hackers. The Trump administration has begun the process of limiting visas to potential foreign agents seeking jobs in academia, science, or technology.

Another aggressive move by the White House was to impose the tariffs that President Obama merely threatened. In early 2018, Trump placed tariffs on $50 billion worth of Chinese imports into America. The tariffs were part of larger efforts on Trump's part to make America's economic relationship with China healthier. The tariffs were part of an escalating trade negotiation that resulted in a "phase one" agreement with Beijing in late 2019, one that currently sits precariously in flux as consumers await a more final deal.

21.

TRUMP KILLED NET NEUTRALITY AND BROADBAND SPEEDS IN AMERICA IMPROVED BY 35.8 PERCENT

The leftist media said killing net neutrality would bring the Internet screeching to a halt. In fact, the opposite happened.

However you feel about the Internet and Silicon Valley, the mass medium and its masters are indisputably a large part of your life. The successful effort to dismantle net neutrality and stop its being used as a political cudgel is among one of Donald Trump's major victories over the deep state. Don't worry, this chapter won't bore you to tears with technical minutiae. After all, the intent of this tome is to wake you from a coma, not put you into one. Wrapping your brain around what net neutrality is, why Trump killed it, and what effect it had on the Internet before he did is critical to understanding the Trump playbook on defeating big government policies.

Net neutrality is unusual compared to the vast majority of Trump's victories because so few Americans actually know what it was. To briefly summarize, net neutrality was the ultimate achievement of President Obama's Internet policy. Developed to help his BFFs at Google and Facebook, if not written directly by the Internet giants themselves, net neutrality was a scheme that allowed the Federal Communications Commission (FCC) to place burdensome regulations on Internet service providers (ISPs).

Under net neutrality, ISPs were forced to treat all Internet traffic the same and they could not charge Internet companies to fasttrack their bandwidth-clogging content. So, if, for example, an ISP's servers were clogged with Millennials streaming *Stranger Things* on Netflix, or Zoomers (Generation Z-ers) watching endless YouTube videos, the ISPs couldn't touch the Silicon Valley Masters of the Universe or attempt to make a profit on their efforts and investments— you know, the whole point of capitalism.

Net neutrality was foisted on the American people in a masterful work of marketing misdirection. We were told that the point of the program and its regulations was to protect a "free and open Internet" and to prevent the evil ISPs from censoring speech or overcharging for Internet access. There's just one problem. Net neutrality was the answer to a problem that didn't exist. There simply isn't an ocean of examples of ISPs censoring the Internet that didn't turn out to be minor mistakes or temporary flukes. Like most big government boondoggles, net neutrality did the exact opposite of what it claimed to do. Instead of ensuring a "free and open Internet," it put even more power in the hands of Silicon Valley monopolies like Google and Facebook, the most censorious companies online. The fatal flaw of net neutrality in this regard is that it focused only on the ISPs, while tech companies like YouTube were left free to censor users and shut down channels. Find any conservative voice that has been snuffed out by Google or a social media platform and ask them if they've faced more censorship from Silicon Valley giants like Twitter and YouTube or from Comcast and other ISPs. I can safely predict they will tell you it's billionaire creeps in California who cause all the problems, not the companies that run the "Internet tubes," as young people like to call them.

Somehow, the left conveniently forgot that the Internet worked wonderfully for several decades before net neutrality. Take, for example, Facebook CEO Mark Zuckerberg. He testified to Congress in April 2018 that Facebook might not exist without net neutrality, claiming, "When I was building Facebook at Harvard I only had one option for an ISP to use and if I had to pay extra in order to make it that my app could potentially be seen or used by other people then we wouldn't probably be here today."

His argument may make you pause and think for a moment. *Maybe Jerome is barking up the wrong tree if Zuckerberg says Facebook wouldn't exist without net neutrality.* But there's just one problem with Zuckerberg's logic. Facebook was founded nearly a decade *before* net neutrality became law. The college dropout built his billion-dollar company under the old Internet system, which worked just fine for everyone. It was only after Zuckerberg and his fellow Silicon Valley tycoons amassed their power that they advocated for control over the Internet, controls that would benefit them first and foremost.

Donald Trump signed net neutrality's death warrant when he nominated Ajit Pai as chairman of the FCC. Pai made his disdain of net neutrality clear from the start. He intended to kill it and return the Internet to its rightful place. Pai saw right through the Silicon Valley lobbyists and their Democratic allies. He said, "They might cloak their advocacy in the public interest, but the real interest of these Internet giants is in using the regulatory process to cement their dominance in the Internet economy."

Pai was not concerned about censorship by ISPs or these providers gouging their customers by devising devilish pricing tiers or charging more to access Netflix. In fact, if ISPs are the Internet pipe and we are at the receiving end, Pai argued that practically all the censorship was at the other end. Pai used the technical term "edge providers" to describe companies that, like Google, Facebook, Twitter, and Apple, send us content through the ISPs. Instead of summarizing Pai's piercing thoughts on the real problems of censorship on the Internet, I will quote him on the matter:

> **[Edge] providers routinely block or discriminate against content they don't like. . . . The examples from the past year alone are legion. App stores barring the doors to apps from even cigar aficionados because they are perceived to promote tobacco use. Streaming services restricting videos from the likes of conservative commentator Dennis Prager on subjects he considers "important to understanding American values." Algorithms that decide what content you see (or don't), but aren't disclosed themselves. Online platforms secretly editing certain users' comments. And of course, American companies caving to repressive foreign governments' demands to block certain speech—conduct that would be repugnant to free expression if it occurred within our borders.**
>
> **In this way, edge providers are a much bigger actual**

threat to an open Internet than broadband providers, especially when it comes to discrimination on the basis of viewpoint.

In late 2017, Pai made his plans to repeal net neutrality public. Predictably, all hell broke loose on the left. Besides the outrage in Silicon Valley, practically every Hollywood star suddenly became an expert on how the Internet works.

Net Neutrality Tweets

"EVERYONE should care about this! It benefits no one unless you're a faceless, mega corporation. NOBODY is asking for it," *Avengers: Endgame* star Chris Evans shrieked.

"#FUCKtheFCC," actress Rosie O'Donnell tweeted.

"Trump wants to kill net neutrality and limit our online content choices. Probably thinks it will help out the VCR industry," *Star Trek* actor George Takei furiously tweeted.

Plastic surgery aficionado Cher offered her standard, over-the-top all-caps screeching on the subject: "Net Neutrality means Trump can Change the Internet!! It Will Include LESS AMERICANS NOT MORE!! Now Comcast, AT&T, Google Will show you ONLY WHAT THEY WANT YOU TO SEE!! SLOWER AND MORE EXPENSIVE AT THEIR WHIM!! SEE LESS, CHARGED MORE . . ."

Senator Bernie Sanders (I-VT) warned that "this is the end of the Internet as we know it." Again, the FCC neutrality regulations were only in place for *two* years!

Burger King, perhaps the last company you'd expect to see jump into a political debate, aired commercials defending net neutrality. The commercials imagined a world where ordering a Whopper was similar to the left's nightmare visions of the Internet's future: consumers forced to pay dramatically higher prices to get their sandwich fast and hot. Christie-Lee McNally, the director of Free Our Internet, an anti–net neutrality group, had sharp words for the burger joint. "Perhaps Burger King's time would be better spent on working to reduce the 36 percent obesity rate in this country rather than hawking its 37g fat-Whopper under the guise of 'net neutrality.'"

The hysteria was all a cynical effort by Silicon Valley and their mammoth marketing friends to not give up the power they had been gifted by the Obama administration to run the Internet however they pleased. In front of the cameras, it was all "the sky is falling!" But behind closed doors, leftists in Silicon Valley were singing a slightly different tune.

Take, for example, Google, the most powerful Internet company on the planet. Breitbart Tech exclusively obtained a recording of an all-hands meeting following the 2016 election that includes executives choking back tears over Trump's victory. Google VP Kent Walker angrily proclaimed that nationalism and the looming Trump presidency must become a "blip," or a "hiccup" instead of the beginning of a new political era. But on the tape Walker did something else. He communicated to his company a message meant to mollify his flock on net neutrality going forward. Remember, publicly Google was bemoaning the potential end of net neutrality as something that would forever damage if not kill Internet freedom. But look at how Walker answered a question on the subject to the audience of Google employees who were wondering what Google would do if net neutrality was repealed:

> **On net neutrality, we are hoping that the tradition we have established over the last ten, maybe twenty years of no improper interference in the flow of data takes on a life of its own after a period of time and it forces the public opinion and makes it harder and harder for carriers to improperly interfere in what people are able to see.**

Walker's point was that the Internet was always free and the pressure of this tradition and consumer expectation will keep ISPs from censoring content or charging outrageous extra fees to access Google or any other content provider.

So, Donald Trump's FCC chairman, Ajit Pai, killed net neutrality after it had been law for roughly two years. CNN reported it as "The End of the Internet as We Know It." Of course repealing net neutrality regulations didn't cause widespread gloom and doom. The Internet continues to grow, and the ISPs aren't censoring anyone. On the contrary, the censorship growing by the day comes from the very Silicon Valley tech gods who would have used net neutrality to cement their stranglehold on the entire web.

We also haven't seen the terrible price increases for consumers forecast by Democrats and, um . . . Burger King. In fact, consumers have enjoyed a big win in the death of net neutrality. That came thanks to another prediction by Ajit Pai. He argued that if ISPs had the FCC assurances that they could make good profits by expanding their Internet coverage, they would be incentivized to bury cables, build out infrastructure, and make the million other tech magic moves needed to bring faster Internet to more Americans. Like all his other predictions and opinions, Pai was 100 percent correct on this point.

Just one year after the repeal of net neutrality, Internet speed-test company Ookla announced that broadband speeds in America improved by 35.8 percent. Upload speeds improved by 22 percent. According to Ookla, "As ISPs continue to build out their fiber networks and gigabit-level speeds expand we only expect to see internet speeds increase across the U.S."

Pai was right about the Internet speeding up after the repeal of net neutrality and the left was wrong about, well, everything. Whatever you are using the Internet for today, whether it is gaming, streaming, or reading Breitbart.com, take a moment to thank Ajit Pai and Donald Trump not only for speeding up the Internet but also for protecting its status as a free and open marketplace and not the playpen of Silicon Valley busybodies.

22.

TRUMP CONFIRMED A HISTORIC NUMBER OF JUDGES

President Trump has confirmed a historic number of judges to the federal judiciary, a sweeping sea change to the nation's courts that will shape his legacy and the country for decades. The president, with the help of Senate Majority Leader Mitch McConnell (R-KY) and a Republican-controlled Senate, confirmed at least 193 judges to the federal bench in the first three years of his tenure. Not to mention the historic confirmations of Brett Kavanaugh and Neil Gorsuch to the Supreme Court. One in four federal circuit judges are now Trump appointees.

The historic number of appointments to the circuit court is even more impressive considering that the average age of the circuit judges is less than fifty years old, which is ten years younger than the average age of President Obama's circuit appointees. The record-breaking pace of Trump's courts of appeal judicial appointments—fifty as of early 2020—far exceeded that of former president Barack Obama's fifty-five total circuit court appointments during his entire presidency.

In November 2019, the U.S. Court of Appeals for the Eleventh

Circuit flipped from a majority of Democrat appointees to a Republican majority. Many other federal courts have followed a similar track, controlled by conservative judges. By February 2020, Trump had "effectively flipped the circuit," said Ninth Circuit Judge Milan D. Smith Jr. about the president's makeover of the San Francisco–based circuit, which covers California and eight other states. One of Trump's Ninth Circuit appointees is Patrick Bumatay, an openly gay Filipino American (the second openly gay judge—the first was Mary Margaret Rowland—Trump had placed on the federal bench in his short time in office).

President Trump said in November 2019, "In terms of quality and quantity, we are going to be just about No. 1 by the time we finish—No. 1 of any president, any administration." The Trump White House said that the Second Circuit, which covers Connecticut, New York, and Vermont, would likely flip to Republican control by the end of 2020. Trump's breakneck ability to fill judicial vacancies is incredibly consequential considering that, although the Supreme Court makes the final decision on court cases, the Supreme Court accepts and rules on about 1 percent of all the cases that are brought before its justices. This means that the increasingly Trump-appointee–controlled Circuit Court of Appeals—which sits one rung below the Supreme Court—has more influence over the vast majority of cases going through the country's federal courts. No small feat, Trump has overwhelmingly appointed judges with an originalist view of the Constitution, who've shown a willingness to refrain from creating law while on the federal bench. President Trump's judges have also shown a propensity to endeavor to undo the work of activist justices who often institute nationwide injunctions against him.

The Trump White House contends that these activist judges often block the administration from enforcing the law and that nationwide injunctions are a modern invention with no basis in the Constitution.

Democrat-nominated judges blocked several Trump policy initiatives, including his travel ban from terror-ridden countries in the Middle East, his order on detaining illegal immigrants, and a rule that would require that immigrants prove that they either have or can pay for health insurance. To that end, Representative Mark Meadows (R-NC) and Senator Tom Cotton (R-AK) introduced a bill that would prevent circuit courts from blocking policy changes handed down by activist judges. Indeed, some of the president's early appointees quickly sent shock waves through the court, derailing an expansion of gender ideology far outside the mainstream.

Judge Stuart Kyle Duncan, a member of the fifth U.S. Circuit of Appeals appointed by Trump, issued an advisory opinion in January 2020 that dismissed a transgender defendant's chosen pronouns and the broader concept of "gender identity." Norman Varner, now a transgender person named Kathrine Nicole Jett, pleaded guilty in 2012 to attempted receipt of child pornography, then moved to have the conviction records updated to match his new name. Duncan referred to Jett using only "he" pronouns and called him a "gender-dysphoric person," instead of using the politically correct term "transgender person."

NBC News even attempted to smear some of President Trump's court appointees as anti-gay by citing a leftist LGBT advocacy group, Lambda Legal. The leftist online outlet *Vox* noted that although there remains no objective way to measure legal ability, President Trump's appointees have more impressive legal credentials compared to Obama's nominees. *Vox*'s Ian Millhiser wrote that roughly 40 percent of President Trump's appellate nominees clerked for a Supreme Court justice, and approximately 80 percent clerked on a federal court of appeals. In contrast, less than one-quarter of Obama appointees clerked on the Supreme Court, and less than half of those nominees worked on a federal appeals court. When Justice Sonia Sotomayor was a lower court judge, she said, "The court of appeals is where policy is made."

Millhiser noted that President Trump's judges will have influence that will extend far beyond his presidency. "Trump's nominees will serve for years or even decades after being appointed. Even if Democrats crush the 2020 elections and win majorities in both houses of Congress, these judges will have broad authority to sabotage the new president's agenda," Millhiser explained. "There is simply no recent precedent for one president having such a transformative impact on the courts."

Senate Democrats, having been resigned to the minority since 2015, have been left impotent in the face of the flood of Trump-appointed judges. Senate Minority Leader Chuck Schumer (D-NY) said that Democrats have done "everything we can" to slow down the confirmation of federal judges. However, McConnell reduced the debate time for a judicial confirmation from thirty hours to just two, making confirmation of judges much more streamlined. Former Senate Minority Leader Harry Reid's (D-NV) elimination of the filibuster rule allowed Republicans to appoint a slew of Supreme Court justices and federal court judges. Democrats controlled the Senate for less than 14 months after Reid eliminated the filibuster rule on federal judges. This has allowed the Republican-controlled Senate as well as President Trump to nominate and confirm a historic number of judges to the federal bench, shifting the balance of the court for years and even decades to come. McConnell noted that President Trump has appointed fifty circuit court judges, which "is already the most in any president's whole first term since 1980."

Christopher Kang, chief counsel at the leftist advocacy group Demand Justice, contended that Trump's historic number of judicial confirmations is the untold success story of the Trump presidency. "While all eyes were understandably on impeachment, Mitch McConnell's conveyor belt churned out a shocking number of judges this week in what remains the most underrated story of the Trump era," Kang said.

President Trump confirmed so many judges during his first term that leading leftist groups sent a letter to McConnell and Senate Judiciary Committee Chairman Lindsey Graham (R-SC) urging them to stop confirming judges while Trump was being impeached by House Democrats. "As long as the cloud of impeachment exists, it would be a grave mistake for the Senate to allow the president to continue making lifetime appointments to the federal judiciary," the leftist groups wrote.

President Trump celebrated his historic confirmations in trademark fashion in a January 2020 tweet. "Now up to 187 Federal Judges, and two great new Supreme Court Justices. We are in major record territory. Hope EVERYONE is happy!"

23.

TRUMP DISMANTLED IRAN'S OBAMA-FUNDED WAR MACHINE

It was perhaps the defining image of Obama-era foreign policy: ten American sailors in navy fatigues, kneeling with their hands behind their heads, held at gunpoint by the Islamic Revolutionary Guard Corps (IRGC). Now considered a terrorist organization, the IRGC is a formal branch of the Iranian military, and the one tasked with most acts of belligerence against the United States. In January 2016, the IRGC seized two U.S. Navy patrol ships in the Persian Gulf and subjected the soldiers to what the navy later described as "aggressive" behavior, intimidating them into divulging passwords for technology on the ships and other key information.

It was the night of Barack Obama's final State of the Union address.

The abduction lasted about 24 hours before Iran freed the soldiers, but the damage was done. Iran had enough ammunition for propaganda declaring that it had bested the greatest military on earth.

"Iran frees trespassing US sailors after Americans apologized," the Iranian state outlet PressTV blared following their release, insisting that the soldiers had been forced to apologize for allegedly navigating into Iranian waters. "After technical and operational examinations done in interaction with the country's relevant political and national security authorities and the establishment of the inadvertent and unintentional nature of the entry by the American Navy crafts and their apology, a decision was made to free them," the IRGC claimed.

PressTV ran several photos of the soldiers apparently sitting in a line on a red carpet, which the Iranian state claimed proved that the soldiers were treated well. The photos were "a reflection of the real Islam and a lesson for the whole world," one Iranian lawmaker claimed.

Later that month, Iran threw a military parade. In April, Qasem Soleimani—the head of the IRGC's Quds Force, the external terrorism command—flew to Moscow, which international sanctions banned him from doing, suffering no consequences. By August 2016, Iran's maritime harassment brigades had nearly doubled the number of belligerent interactions with American naval ships in the Gulf from the first eight months of 2015.

Iran's Global Influence

Looking back after a full term of Donald Trump, it is difficult to grasp just how powerful the Obama administration had made Iran. The Obama White House promised Americans that enriching and supporting the ayatollahs would result in Iran liking us, locking up its "death to America" posters, and becoming a free country. Instead, Iran took our money and invested it immediately in our destruction.

By 2016, Iran was on the rise, increasingly influential not just in Syria—where Soleimani had spent months helping dictator Bashar al-Assad crush civilians to stay in power—but in Iraq, where the Shiite government of Baghdad was reaching out for help against ISIS, and in Yemen, where the Shiite Houthi rebel organization had decided it was time to overthrow the legitimate Sunni government a year after its allies in Tehran had begun to benefit from the nuclear deal with the West. In Lebanon, Hezbollah—yet another, more openly terrorist proxy organization allied with Iran—was gaining ground and fueling chaos amid protests against Beirut's impotent government. Across the globe in Venezuela, Tareck El Aissami, the Lebanese-Syrian governor of Aragua state, was gaining prominence in an increasingly unstable game of musical chairs behind dictator Nicolás Maduro. In Argentina, a top prosecutor who had compiled hundreds of pages of evidence showing the leftist government of former president Cristina Fernández de Kirchner pressuring Interpol to protect Iranian terrorists mysteriously "committed suicide," effectively ending the investigation.

President Obama's foreign policy was indisputably to blame for this fast-tracked ascent in global influence on the part of the Islamic regime. As part of the nuclear deal—formally the Joint

Comprehensive Plan of Action (JCPoA)—Obama and the other guarantor nations had lifted onerous sanctions meant to prevent Tehran from selling oil to fund its terrorist activities. Obama packed some other goodies in the deal, too, like a $1.7 billion ransom-that-was-not-a-ransom for the freedom of several American hostages and $150 billion in funds frozen in response to Iranian terrorism.

The Obama administration routinely lied, by its admission, to convince Americans that giving that money away would lead to peace. The failed novelist running Obama's foreign policy, Ben Rhodes, admitted in the tail end of his tenure that everything the White House claimed about President Hassan Rouhani being a moderate was fiction, but necessary spin to advance the righteous goal of making the repressors of the Iranian people filthy rich. Secretary of State John Kerry openly admitted the Iran deal would fund terrorism.

When President Trump took office in 2017, he faced one of the most complex foreign policy scenarios of any president. The Middle East, with a Syrian war theater hosting as many as ten different armed forces fighting each other at once, was a particular challenge, exacerbated by the newly emboldened Iran. Trump campaigned on getting rid of the Iran nuclear deal and restoring sanctions, which he did in 2018.

Giving up the nuclear deal and limiting Iran's access to global markets, which it used to fund its terrorism, solved only part of the problem, and slowly at that. Iran still had its windfall from the Obama era and used it to fund Hezbollah and, of course, its more formal twin, the IRGC. Iran also has its vast oil reserves, which it uses to generate funding by selling oil to much of Europe and Asia.

President Trump addressed the latter with sanctions directly on

Iran's oil industry and corresponding pressure on European nations and Asian allies like Japan and India to stop buying. The sanctions had a dual effect: limiting Iran's access to terrorism funding and bolstering sales of U.S. oil to nations seeking to fill the void left by Iran's fuel.

Trump also took the unprecedented step of formally designating the IRGC a terrorist organization, the first official wing of a foreign military to fall into that category.

"This action will significantly expand the scope and scale of our maximum pressure on the Iranian regime. It makes crystal clear the risks of conducting business with, or providing support to, the IRGC," Trump said in a statement in April 2019, announcing the designation. "If you are doing business with the IRGC, you will be bankrolling terrorism."

The designation essentially allowed the White House to treat the IRGC not as a foreign army, but as a terrorist group, indistinguishable from the Islamic State or al-Qaeda. It also cut Iran off from the giant megaphones it had built on American social media to spread its violent, anti-American propaganda. Particularly injurious to the ego of Quds Force chief Soleimani was Instagram's decision to delete his page, popular at the time with Shiite jihadists.

Not all lauded the success of Trump's strategy. "Trump sanctions on Iran have done nothing to change Iranian behavior except make it worse," Ben Rhodes grumbled. The *Financial Times* predicted the ever-popular Soleimani would soon become president. The reality for Soleimani and his cohort was far more dire.

"In March, Hezbollah's leader, Hassan Nasrallah, went on TV and made a public appeal for donations," Brian Hook, the U.S. Special Representative for Iran, told Congress in June 2019. "Hezbollah has placed piggy banks in grocery stores and in retail outlets seeking the spare change of people."

By February 2020, an impotent Nasrallah was using his time on Iranian state television to demand that all Hezbollah members boycott the United States, no longer purchasing American products or traveling there. As Hezbollah is a designated terrorist organization, its members are not allowed to roam freely in America, anyway, and few in Iran, Lebanon, Syria, or Iraq are likely to have access to the American market.

Lebanese people online responded to the boycott with mockery, sharing a photo of the one person tied to Hezbollah who did appear to enjoy American products: Nasrallah's son, decked in a Timberland hoodie.

As for Qasem Soleimani, he never got to live up to the promise the *Financial Times* saw in him to become the next Iranian president. Trump ordered his execution via drone strike in January 2020. Soleimani was a general in a foreign regime, yes, but more importantly a senior member of the IRGC, a foreign terrorist organization, making his execution legally comparable to that of ISIS chief Abu Bakr al-Baghdadi.

A week before his demise at an airport in Baghdad, Soleimani had been active in Iraq organizing Shiite jihadists to attack American troops. Soleimani had pioneered the use of roadside bombs to kill and dismember Americans, racking up hundreds of American casualties.

Days before the airstrike that killed him, a mob of angry jihadists scribbled "Soleimani is our commander" on the walls of the American embassy in Baghdad.

24.

AMERICA BECAME A NET EXPORTER OF NATURAL GAS AND CRUDE OIL FOR THE FIRST TIME IN MORE THAN FIFTY YEARS

The Trump administration has championed the responsible culti-vation of America's plentiful energy resources, including oil and natural gas. The president's policy positions, as such, have been geared toward expanding oil drilling and natural gas exploitation as a means to boost the country's economy, save Americans money through lower energy prices, and increase America's national secu-rity through reduced dependence on foreign oil.

Much of America's energy boom during Trump's tenure can be attributed to his stated strategy of "energy dominance." The White House's Council of Economic Advisers (CEA) 2020 report found that in 2017 the United States became a net exporter of natural gas. It was a feat not seen since 1958. Further amplifying Trump's suc-cess in boosting America's energy boom, the United States became a net exporter of crude oil and petroleum products and will likely remain a net exporter for all of 2020 for the first time since 1949.

The CEA contended that the country's growth and dominance in the fossil fuel sector has boosted the economy and has fortified national security. "The innovation-driven surge in production and exports has made the U.S. economy more resilient to global price spikes. It has also improved the country's geopolitical flexibility and influence, as evidenced by concurrent sanctions on two major oil-producing countries, Iran and Venezuela," the CEA report said.

The U.S. Energy Information Administration (EIA) forecast in January 2020 that American natural gas exports will almost double by 2021 to an average of 7.3 billion cubic feet per day. The EIA said that the growth in U.S. net exports has been led primarily by increases in liquefied natural gas (LNG) and pipeline exports to Mexico. The federal energy agency also noted that in 2019 "growth in demand for U.S. natural gas exports exceeded growth in natural gas consumption in the U.S. electric power sector." The explosion in natural gas has lowered American energy prices, leaving more Americans with more money to save and invest in their future.

The CEA found that the shale revolution in natural gas has saved American consumers $203 billion every year, which amounts to an average of $2,500 in savings for a family of four.

"Nearly 80 percent of the savings stem from a substantially lower price for natural gas, of which more than half comes through lower electricity prices," the CEA said.

The economic adviser group also noted that the reduction in energy prices has especially helped America's lower-income families. "Because lower-income households, spend a larger share of their income on energy bills, the savings have greater relative importance for them," the Council of Economic Advisers wrote. "Energy savings represent 6.8 percent of income for the lowest fifth of households, compared with 1.3 percent for the highest fifth. In other words, lower energy prices are like a progressive tax cut that helps the lowest households the most."

The explosion in natural gas exports has not only helped American economic well-being and national security, but also it has helped the country reduce its carbon dioxide emissions to a level not previously thought possible.

"In its 2006 Annual Energy Outlook, the EIA projected a 16.5 percent increase in carbon dioxide emissions from 2005 to 2018. Actual emissions decreased by about 12 percent. Actual energy-related carbon emissions for 2018 were 24 percent lower than projected in 2006," the CEA explained. "Some of the decline is because projections assumed greater GDP growth and therefore greater electricity demand than what actually occurred, in part because of the Great Recession and slow recovery. An important part of the decline, however, stems from lower natural gas prices reducing reliance on electricity generated from coal. Over the period, the proportion of generation from coal-fired power plants fell from 50 percent to 28 percent, while the share from natural gas increased from 19 percent to 35 percent."

The United States' production in natural gas has even enabled the country to reduce total greenhouse gas (GHG) emissions faster than the entire European Union (EU). This is even more outstanding considering that the EU developed and expanded an "increasingly stringent cap-and-trade" climate change program across the bloc of nations. "Although it substantially raised electricity prices for consumers . . . the system helped the European Union achieve a 20 percent decline in GDP-adjusted emissions from 2005 to 2017, the most recent year of data," the White House CEA revealed. "Over the same period, emissions fell by 28 percent in the United States, which did not implement a national cap-and-trade system, although various States have pursued policies to cap emissions."

The expansion of natural gas production has largely been a product of hydraulic fracturing, more commonly known as fracking. Most states allow fracking; however, Maryland, Vermont, and New York have banned it.

New York and Pennsylvania have shale natural gas resources; however, New York has not benefited from the nationwide fracking revolution. "The difference in energy-related outcomes in the two States is stark. Development of the Marcellus and Utica Shale in Pennsylvania caused natural gas production to increase 10-fold from 2010 to 2017. Over the same period, New York's production fell by nearly 70 percent. Pennsylvania leads the country in net exports of electricity to other States and produces more than twice the amount of energy it consumes," a CEA report noted. "New York, in contrast, has grown more dependent on electricity generated elsewhere; and in 2017, the State consumed four times as much energy as it produced. Despite the growth in energy production in Pennsylvania, total energy-related carbon dioxide emissions fell 15 percent from 2010 to 2016, the most recent year of data, twice as much as in New York (7 percent). The greater decline in Pennsylvania stems from larger reductions in the electric power sector."

Further, the Trump administration has doubled the volume of LNG for export, which has nearly doubled the capacity to sell across the world as of October 2019. "The Trump Administration's deregulatory policies aim to support private sector innovation and initiative by reducing excessively prescriptive government regulation. In doing so, the Administration seeks to further unleash the country's abundant human and energy resources," the CEA said.

25.

FOR THE FIRST TIME EVER, THERE WERE MORE JOB OPENINGS IN EARLY 2020 THAN PEOPLE LOOKING FOR WORK

When Donald Trump ran for president, he promised to reinvigorate the economy and get Americans back to work. He vowed to end the dismal economic growth of Barack Obama's presidency and enact policies that would unshackle the country's economic engine. Since President Trump took the oath of office, the stock market, wages, and employment have all skyrocketed. The economy improved so well for American workers that Trump achieved a victory that no other president in modern American history has accomplished. For the first time on record, job openings have exceeded those looking for work, with one million more openings than job seekers at the end of 2019.

"We will get our people off of welfare and back to work—rebuilding our country with American hands and American labor," President Trump said during his inaugural address, making a commitment to restoring the country and putting Americans back to work. "We will follow two simple rules: Buy American and hire American."

NUMBER OF UNEMPLOYED PEOPLE VERSUS NUMBER OF JOB OPENINGS, 2001–2019

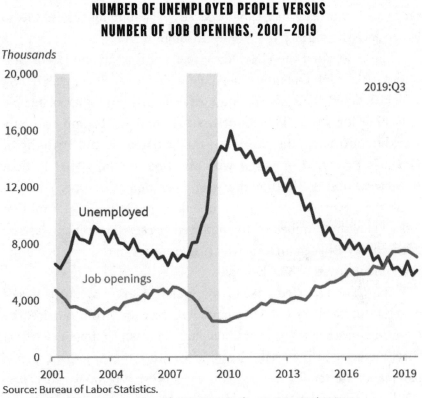

Source: Bureau of Labor Statistics.
Note: Shading denotes a recession. The JOLTS series began in December 2000.

The rise in employment and job openings especially benefits the lives of so-called discouraged workers, or those who have simply given up looking for work due to the economic constraints of the Obama administration. The White House Council of Economic

Advisers (CEA) wrote in their February 2020 report that the Trump economy is "also encouraging those individuals to put themselves back in the workforce. My Administration has placed a special focus on those forgotten Americans because every individual deserves to experience the dignity that comes through work."

The CEA cited the U.S. Department of Bureau and Labor Statistics' (BLS) Job Openings and Labor Turnover Survey (JOLTS), which detailed that job openings exceeded the number of people searching for work. The council wrote that the Trump economy starkly contrasted the economy that existed at the twilight of Obama's tenure. "Compared with the time of the 2016 election, there were over 1.4 million more job openings in October 2019. In total, there were 7.3 million job openings in October—1.4 million more than the number of unemployed persons. October was the 20th consecutive month in which there were more job openings than unemployed," the CEA said.

The CEA reported that in the fourth quarter of 2019, three-quarters of workers entering employment came from outside the labor force rather than from unemployment, which amounts to the "highest share in the series' history." In 2019, the American unemployment rate fell to 3.5 percent, the lowest rate in five decades. "Falling unemployment has reduced the share of the population on unemployment insurance to the lowest level since recording started in 1967," the CEA noted.

Trump's record of economic growth means that Americans across several communities and demographics have been uplifted. In 2018, 1.4 million Americans were lifted out of poverty, and the American poverty rate decreased to the lowest level since 2001. The poverty rates for black and Hispanic Americans hit historic lows. Black Americans saw dramatic increases in employment and earnings over 2019. The employment-population ratio for prime working-age black Americans grew from 75.1 percent to 77.2 percent from 2018 to 2019. The black unemployment rate hit a record low of 5.4 percent in August 2019, and the weekly earnings of black full-time workers rose 4.3 percent after adjusting for inflation.

The CEA noted that the nominal wage growth for black Americans has risen dramatically, explaining, "While nominal wage growth for all private-sector workers has been at or above 3 percent for all but one month in 2019, wage growth for many historically disadvantaged groups is now higher than wage growth for more advantaged groups, as is the case for lower-income workers compared with higher-income ones, for workers compared with managers, and for African Americans compared with whites. These income gains mark a fundamental change relative to those opposite trends observed over the expansion before President Trump's inauguration, contributing to reduced income inequality." The poverty rate for single mothers and children had also fallen "much faster than the average."

"Since [President Trump] took office, food insecurity has fallen, and nearly 7 million people have been lifted off food stamps. Beneficiaries entering the labor market or increasing their incomes through work is likely driving falling enrollment in Medicaid, TANF, and disability insurance," the CEA added.

The dynamic economic growth Americans experienced can be attributed to President Donald Trump's advocacy for sweeping tax reform through the Tax Cuts and Jobs Act, which enacted the most significant tax reform in decades. "Since the Tax Cuts and Jobs Act— the biggest package of tax cuts and tax reforms in our country's history—took effect, more than 4 million jobs have been created, and economic growth has beaten previous projections," the CEA wrote. The Council of Economic Advisers also noted that, since Trump took office, the economy had added more than seven million jobs, which far exceeds the 1.9 million new jobs predicted by the Congressional Budget Office (CBO).

The Trump economic boom also applies to working-class Americans and those with disabilities. The unemployment rate for Americans without a high school degree declined to 4.8 percent in September 2019, the lowest percentage point on record since 1992. "Since the President's election, the unemployment rate for those without a high school degree has fallen at a faster rate than the rate for those with a bachelor's degree or higher. The gap between the two rates reached a series low under the Trump Administration," the CEA noted. "For people with a high school degree but not a college education, the unemployment rate fell to 3.4 percent in April 2019, the lowest it has been in over 18 years. And for individuals with some college experience but no bachelor's degree the rate fell to 2.7 percent in December 2019, the lowest since 2001."

The CEA said about veterans and disabled Americans, "Persons with disabilities can have a harder time finding work, as can veterans. However, President Trump's policies are translating into economic gains for these populations as well. In September 2019, the unemployment rate for persons with a disability dropped to 6.1 percent, the lowest it has been since the series began in 2008. In April 2019, the unemployment rate for American veterans fell to 2.3 percent, matching the series low previously achieved in 2000."

26.

THE POVERTY RATE FOR BLACK AND HISPANIC AMERICANS DROPPED TO AN ALL-TIME LOW IN 2018

The poverty rate for black Americans fell by 0.9 percentage points and by 0.8 percentage points for Hispanic Americans in 2018, the latest year for which data is available. Those figures represent, for both groups, the lowest levels of poverty ever recorded by the Census Bureau. The poverty rates for both groups also hit record lows the previous year, with black poverty rates falling to 21.2 percent and 18.3 for Hispanics in 2017. The rate was expected by experts to fall to another historic low in 2019. That defies the Democrats' chorus of doom and gloom about the economy. Just a few months after the Census Bureau reported record-breaking poverty declines, a Gallup survey assessing the economic mood of the nation found that 59 percent of Americans said they are better off financially than they were just a year earlier—and a staggering 74 percent said they will be even better off in 2020.

The measure of poverty peaked for black Americans at 41.8 percent in 1966, the year the Census Bureau issued its first report measuring poverty among American families. The number peaked at

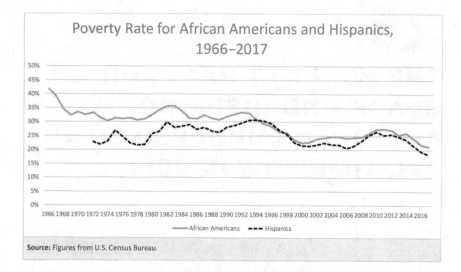

Poverty Rate for African Americans and Hispanics, 1966–2017

Source: Figures from U.S. Census Bureau.

30.7 for Hispanics in 1994. Developed in the early 1960s by Mollie Orshansky, a staff economist at the Social Security Administration, the government's official measure of poverty is derived from "money income thresholds that vary by family size and composition to determine who is in poverty. If a family's total income is less than the family's threshold, then that family and every individual in it is considered in poverty."

Post–World War II history saw the poverty rate in America nose-dive decades before President Lyndon Johnson launched his Great Society programs, dramatically expanding the nation's welfare state through social engineering and wealth redistribution. In 1950, the American poverty rate was 32.2 percent. By 1965, that number had fallen by nearly half to 17.3 percent without any sweeping government intervention. That is no less than an American miracle. In 2018, again, with the latest data available, the overall poverty rate in America stood at 11.8 percent or roughly 38 million people. Poverty in America declined for nearly twenty years and fell by roughly 15 percent without a massive welfare state spending spree. But between 1965 and 2018—more than fifty years and after more than $22 trillion in new spending—the poverty rate declined just 5.5 percent. It's a statistical stagnation that only begins to illustrate the abject failure Johnson's Great Society was.

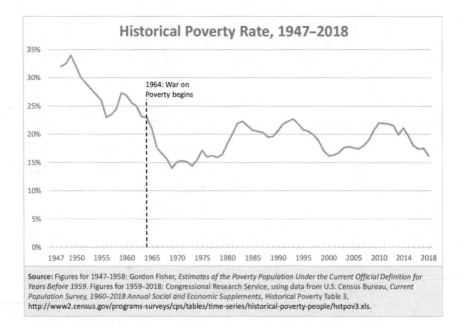

Source: Figures for 1947–1958: Gordon Fisher, *Estimates of the Poverty Population Under the Current Official Definition for Years Before 1959.* Figures for 1959–2018: Congressional Research Service, using data from U.S. Census Bureau, *Current Population Survey, 1960–2018 Annual Social and Economic Supplements*, Historical Poverty Table 3, http://www2.census.gov/programs-surveys/cps/tables/time-series/historical-poverty-people/hstpov3.xls.

The Trump economy also made inroads in decreasing the rate of poverty for those on the margins of the American mainstream. The official poverty rate for those 18 and under fell by 1.2 percentage points in 2018, bringing the rate down to 16.2 percent. Poverty among single mothers with children fell by 2.5 percent.

"As incomes rose, inequality fell. The share of income held by the top 20 percent fell by the largest amount in over a decade, as did the Gini index (an overall measure of inequality in the population)," read a White House Council of Economic Advisers report. "In fact, households between the twentieth and fortieth percentile of the distribution experienced the largest increase in average household income among all quintiles in 2018, with a gain of 2.5 percent."

The economic collapse in 2008 and the devastating recession that followed it pushed people out of the labor force and onto welfare rolls. As the job market slowly began to rebound, and Americans rejoined the labor force, the poverty rate began to dip in 2014. President Trump's laser focus on reviving the economy, lowering taxes, and pushing a mammoth rollback of regulations gave businesses the confidence to hire more workers. "There were 2.3 million more full-time, year-round workers in 2018 than in 2017, of which 1.6 million were women," the report said. "Real median earnings of full-time, year-round workers increased by 3.4 percent ($1,832) among men and by 3.3 percent ($1,439) among women in 2018 compared to the previous year."

27.

EPA CRIMINAL ACTIONS DROPPED TO A THIRTY-YEAR LOW

The Environmental Protection Agency (EPA) was created by President Richard Nixon to help protect and keep clean America's land, air, and water. Nixon charged the federal agency with enforcing the nation's environmental laws and referring violators for criminal prosecution. President Bill Clinton's administration weaponized the agency. Prosecutions skyrocketed. So-called sue-and-settle lawsuits were launched against an array of industries. By the end of President Obama's tenure, the EPA had morphed into an agency so powerful that it made a criminal out of seventy-seven-year-old disabled Navy veteran Joe Robertson, who was slapped with a six-figure fine and an eighteen-month prison sentence for digging ponds on his property on a state permit when he should've done the digging on a federal one.

In contrast, EPA-enforced prosecutions hit a multidecade low under President Donald Trump. The Trump EPA says it concentrates resources toward pursuing the most egregious polluters and is focused on helping industries comply with the nation's environmental laws instead of breaking the backs of businesses that unwittingly run afoul of them. Indeed, pollution-related cases referred for criminal prosecution by the EPA hit a thirty-year low in 2018, according to Department of Justice (DOJ) data. The EPA said in 2019 that it diverted "its resources to the most significant and impactful cases." In 2019, 166 cases were referred for criminal prosecution, the lowest number of cases since 1988, when Ronald Reagan's EPA saw 151 cases referred.

The agency's referrals reached a high of 592 under Clinton in 1998. Since then, the criminal referrals have been on a downward trajectory and have fallen by more than one-fourth since 2016. In 2018, the EPA referrals led to 62 federal convictions, which was the fewest since 1995. An EPA spokesman said the federal agency has still been able to crack down on abusive behavior. The EPA issued $72 million in civil penalties in 2018, which is the lowest level in two decades. This serves as a massive contrast to Obama's final year in office, in which his EPA issued $6 billion in civil fines against corporations.

Susan Bodine, an assistant administrator for the EPA's Office of Enforcement and Compliance Assurance, said that the agency will continue to enforce compliance with environmental regulations. "Let there be no mistake, EPA enforcement will continue to correct non-compliance using all the tools at its disposal, including imposing civil penalties to maintain a level playing field and deter future misconduct."

"Special agents carefully allocate our finite resources by going after the biggest, most serious offenders that affect the most people," an EPA spokeswoman said in an email. "These crimes involve death or serious injury, multiple locations, and large or significant enterprises."

The EPA reported in February 2020 that it has encouraged businesses to self-disclose and correct violations, which led to companies deciding to rectify wrongdoing. "EPA's enforcement program is focused on achieving compliance with environmental laws using all tools available," said Bodine in February 2020. "Our goal is to eliminate inefficient duplication with state programs, and to direct federal resources to help achieve the Agency's core mission of improving air quality, providing for clean and safe water, revitalizing land and preventing contamination, and ensuring the safety of chemicals in the marketplace."

The EPA's 2019 Enforcement and Compliance Achievements

- There were voluntary self-disclosed violations at over 1,900 facilities returned to compliance, an estimated 20 percent increase compared to 2018.
- There was a total of $471.8 million in federal, judicial civil penalties, and criminal fines, the highest of all but four of the past ten years.
- The EPA has made commitments to reduce, treat, or eliminate 347.2 million pounds of pollution, including air, toxins, and water.
- A total of 137 criminal defendants were charged, an increase from 107 in 2018.
- The EPA has made commitments totaling

> **$570.4 million in new cleanup work.**
> - **The EPA has worked to reduce children's exposure to lead. In 2019, the EPA led 117 federal enforcement actions to ensure that renovation contractors, landlords, realtors, and others comply with rules to protect Americans from exposure to lead from lead-based paint.**

Former Trump EPA administrator Scott Pruitt contended that while Obama pushed for onerous climate change proposals such as the Clean Power Plan (CPP) and the Waters of the United States (WOTUS) rule, the Obama-era EPA failed to improve America's air, water, and contaminated sites. "The past administration is viewed as the environmental savior. But when you look at air attainment in this country, we're at 40 percent non-attainment right now on ozone," Pruitt said. "Superfund sites, we have more today than when President Obama came into office. Water infrastructure, you had Flint, and you had Gold King. And . . . the regulations that they issued on carbon, they failed twice. They struck out twice."

The EPA under Pruitt also ended the agency's sue-and-settle practice; Pruitt called the practice "regulation through litigation" and described it as "abusive." During the Obama administration, leftist environmental groups such as the Sierra Club launched a litany of lawsuits to force the EPA and other federal agencies to issue regulations that advanced their climate change agenda. Those groups would sue the EPA and ask the courts to compel the agency to enact new environmental regulations.

Critics contended that the sue-and-settle practice allowed previous EPA administrators to skirt the federal agency's limited rule-making authority. And, of course, the Obama administration used sue-and-settle tactics far more than previous presidential administrations. Obama's EPA sued and settled 137 times during his eight-year tenure, compared to George W. Bush's 66 cases. Bill Clinton's EPA saw just 27 sue-and-settle cases in his second term.

"The days of regulation through litigation are over," said Pruitt in a statement in October 2017. "We will no longer go behind closed doors and use consent decrees and settlement agreements to resolve lawsuits filed against the agency by special interest groups where doing so would circumvent the regulatory process set forth by Congress. Additionally, gone are the days of routinely paying tens of thousands of dollars in attorneys' fees to these groups with which we swiftly settle." Pruitt argued that the sue-and-settle policy undermined states' authority to police environmental violations.

One infamous sue-and-settle regulation, whose estimated annual cost to the power plant industry the EPA pegged at $9.6 billion, was the maximum achievable control technology (MACT) rule that was imposed on utilities. This emissions-reduction rule was established for air toxins released from coal- and oil-fired electric utility power plants. Pruitt warned at the time that it is "the states that have been impacted in this process because there are obligations that states have under various statutes."

William Ruckelshaus, the EPA's first administrator, admitted in 2018 that Pruitt has moved quickly to dismantle the environmental regulatory apparatus established by the agency. "We've spent 40 years putting together an apparatus to protect public health and the environment from a lot of different pollutants. He's pulling that whole apparatus down," Ruckelshaus said.

Current EPA administrator Andrew Wheeler said that the Trump administration would continue to protect the environment while pushing for light-touch regulations that do not harm the economy. "At EPA, we will continue protecting the environment and human health while making smart regulatory decisions that support our economy and help create jobs," Wheeler said in February 2020. "We have finalized 51 deregulatory actions, saving Americans an estimated $6.5 billion in regulatory costs, and we have an additional 45 actions in development projected to save billions more. Under President Trump's leadership, our Nation is on a positive trajectory and will continue to flourish for the foreseeable future for all Americans, and at EPA we will continue the successful path the agency has laid for the past 50 years."

28.

NET NEW WOMEN-OWNED BUSINESSES ADDED PER DAY REACHED A RECORD HIGH IN 2018

The average number of new women-owned businesses opened per day reached a record level in 2018, surging to 1,821. The number held steady in 2019, a year that saw an average of 1,817 businesses owned by women open per day. The data derives from a U.S. Census Bureau Survey of Business Owners and was part of the annual State of Women-Owned Businesses Report, commissioned by American Express. A woman-owned business is defined as any firm that is "at least 51 percent owned, operated and controlled by one or more females," American Express explains.

No ethnic group has seen more business start-ups in recent years than black women. New businesses owned by black women represented the highest rate of growth of any group in the number of new firms between 2018 and 2019. Indeed, black women accounted for 42 percent of net new women business

owners in 2019, which is three times their share of
the female population. In a dizzying irony, the very
subgroup of voters who supported President Trump's
election the least have in this instance benefited
from his stewardship of the economy the most.

"Women of color represent 39 percent of the total female population in the United States but account for 89 percent of the net
new women-owned businesses opened per day (1,625) over the past
year. They are starting tech companies with the potential of scaling
to become unicorns (companies with $1 billion market valuation),
opening local storefronts, joining the gig economy as contractors,
and everything in between," the report said. "Latina/Hispanic
women represent 31 percent of all net new women-owned businesses, which is nearly double their share of the female population
(17 percent)."

It's a remarkable feat, especially when you consider how under-
represented in the larger economy minority women tend to be in
terms of management positions. While accounting for roughly 47
percent of all U.S. employees in 2018, less than 27 percent of all
chief executives and just 40 percent of all managers were women,
according to Bureau of Labor Statistics estimates. Nearly 84 percent
of women in management were white, 10.3 percent were Hispanic,
and just 3.5 percent were black in 2018.

Minority female–run businesses generate an estimated $981
billion in annual revenues and account for some four million new

jobs, according to MarketWatch. Through the Trump era, a majority of women business owners showed optimism about their ability to grow their business year over year. Roughly 58 percent of women entrepreneurs said their revenues would increase in 2018, which was up from the 44 percent who said so in 2017, according to a study by Bank of America.

The American Express study also found that half of all women-owned businesses are concentrated in three industries, including services (e.g., nail and hair salons); healthcare and social assistance (e.g., day care services); and professional, scientific, and technical services (e.g., attorneys, public relations professionals, consultants). The women-backed business boom also extended to *sidepreneurs*, people who are part-time entrepreneurs working less than 20 hours per week to build their businesses. These part-time entrepreneurs, of course, may also be full-time workers. "Between 2014 and 2019, growth in the number of women sidepreneurs was nearly double overall growth in women entrepreneurs: 39 percent compared to 21 percent respectively. Growth in sidepreneurship is higher for women (39 percent) than for all adult sidepreneurs (32 percent)," the American Express report found. "Considering the race and ethnicity of a sidepreneur revealed an even greater contrast," it also noted. "Over the past five years, the growth in sidepreneurs was two times as high for minority women-owned businesses (65 percent) compared to all sidepreneur businesses (32 percent)."

"Many black women founders may be single parents and need to have this dual income to support the household needs," said Dell Gines, author of a Federal Reserve Bank of Kansas City report, *Black Women Business StartUps*. "Because the women are taking care of their families, they need to have a level of confidence before they can make that jump completely. Women who are responsible for their households tend to keep the size of businesses artificially low because they need health insurance from a primary employer and want to make sure everything is absolutely appropriate before taking the jump."

29.

NET NEUTRALITY REPEAL RAISES ANNUAL INCOMES BY $50 BILLION

The Federal Communications Commission (FCC) may not always receive front-page news coverage on any given day; however, it served as the epicenter of a battle between leftists and conservatives over the repeal of net neutrality. Obama FCC chairman Tom Wheeler passed net neutrality in 2015, which effectively recategorized the Internet as a public utility. Critics contended that the rule diminished Internet freedom, while its proponents argued that the regulations would prevent Internet service providers (ISPs) from discriminating.

President Trump's FCC, under Chairman Ajit Pai, passed the Restoring Internet Freedom Order, recategorizing the Internet as an "information service." As Breitbart News reported, the measure requires that ISPs such as Comcast and Verizon "release transparency reports detailing their practices on blocking, throttling, and data prioritization for consumers and businesses." However, the run-up to the FCC's repeal of net neutrality led to all kinds of laughably unserious outrage from the American left.

American Left Outrage at the Repeal of Net Neutrality

Here's a small sample of the rancor that rang out from left-wing precincts:

- **CNN** declared net neutrality's repeal the "End of the Internet as We've Known It" in December 2017.
- **LGBT** groups declared that the repeal of net neutrality an "attack" on their communities.
- **Senator Bernie Sanders (I-VT)** said in December 2017 it would mean the end of "democracy."

Despite the left's apocalyptic predictions over the repeal of net neutrality, the World Wide Web is still spinning and the Internet has continued to grow and prosper and benefit consumers.

The White House Council of Economic Advisers (CEA) released a report in February 2020 that found that the FCC's repeal of net neutrality raised annual incomes by $50 billion. The CEA also found that net neutrality's repeal increased consumer welfare by $40 billion per year. The White House group found that the pricing restrictions imposed as well as the increased government oversight on ISPs led to much of the increased costs associated with net neutrality.

Go figure: More regulations equal more crushing costs. The economic council said that removing regulations on ISPs would reduce costs and increase Americans' access to the web. "Previous research shows that vertical pricing restrictions in broadband significantly reduce the quantity and quality of services received by broadband consumers. Hazlett and Caliskan (2008), for example, looked at 'open access' restrictions that were applied to U.S. Digital Subscriber Line service (DSL) but not Cable Modem (CM) access," the CEA wrote. "They found that three years after restrictions on DSL services were relaxed, in 2003 and 2005, U.S. DSL subscriptions grew by about 31 percent relative to the trend, while U.S. CM subscriptions increased slightly relative to the trend. Average revenue per DSL subscriber fell, while average revenue per CM subscriber was constant (although quality increased). At the same time, DSL and CM subscriptions in Canada, which was not experiencing the regulatory changes, did not increase relative to the trend."

Now that the FCC under Trump has repealed the net neutrality regulations, ISPs have invested and expanded their Internet infrastructure so that more Americans can enjoy the benefits of the Internet. Pai has made bridging the *digital divide*—closing the gap between those with and without the Internet—a cornerstone of his administration.

Roslyn Layton, a scholar at the American Enterprise Institute (AEI) and Trump 2016 FCC transition team member, explained in a February 2020 report that ISPs have started to invest in their networks after net neutrality's repeal. "Proving that internet freedom is alive and well is the fact that the U.S. accounts for more than a quarter of the world's total private investment in broadband networks.

This regime of facilities-based competition, which has characterized the broadband market up to 2015 and its restoration in December 2017, has delivered almost $2 trillion. Capital has flowed into the U.S. from the rest of the world precisely because investors have been allowed to earn a return, and the rules of the game have largely been based on ex-post, evidentiary standards," Layton wrote.

"It was predictable that investment would fall following the imposition of the Title II regulatory regime in 2015 and 2016. Essentially, the 2015 FCC signaled to investors that it would impose price and traffic controls, thereby reducing the flexibility to manage networks efficiently and the value of the network investment," Layton said. "With the misguided regulation removed, investment now exceeds the 2014 level, second only to the boom of 1999–2001.

"The FCC is delivering on Pai's promise of broadband empowerment by removing outdated and misguided regulation, giving the private sector space to innovate, compete, and invest. The media might not cover it, but millions of Americans experience improving broadband networks every day," she said.

The CEA also revealed significant consumer benefits from repealing the Obama FCC's broadband privacy rule. The council found that the repeal of the broadband privacy rule raised incomes by $22 billion annually and lowered broadband prices. In 2017, Congress passed and President Trump signed a resolution of disapproval under the Congressional Review Act to overturn the Obama disapproval rule. After Trump repealed the agency regulation, broadband prices started falling. "Wireless service prices fell at the same time that Congress was considering the resolution of disapproval, and wired Internet prices fell a couple of months later. Both these declines are about $40 per subscriber over the life of the subscription, which is similar to independent estimates of the per-subscriber cost of obtaining personal data consent from retail customers that are the basis for our quantitative analysis," the CEA wrote.

Tech experts have said that Pai's deregulatory actions have served as an unsung story for those who want a freer, cheaper, and consistently reliable Internet. "The Federal Communications Commission (FCC) recently released a list of its accomplishments under Chairman Ajit Pai. It includes over 220 items adopted in 36 meetings, more than twice the number adopted by the prior administration over a similar period, and 80 percent passed with bipartisan support," Layton wrote in February 2020. "The list includes billions of dollars for the build-out of rural broadband and record-breaking spectrum auctions, all unambiguous wins for the American people.

30.

TRUMP PRIORITIZED BREAKING THE CHINESE MONOPOLY ON RARE EARTH ELEMENTS AND THE U.S. IS DIGGING FOR THEM FOR THE FIRST TIME SINCE THE MANHATTAN PROJECT

I was recently speaking about rare earth elements with a science-minded friend. He complained that 80 percent of the reporters covering the topic for the mainstream press are science-illiterate hacks who know absolutely nothing about the topic. I explained to my friend that he was being far too kind; the percentage is more like 95 percent.

It's perfectly reasonable to wonder why you should care about rare earth elements. You're likely more concerned and certainly more familiar with the prices of other elements like gold and silver, but you should care about rare earth elements. The reason is simple: In our technology-centered society, these elements are indispensable. Rare earth elements, which were virtually nonexistent in the lives of our relatives a hundred years ago, are today in every smartphone, every hard drive, and every flat-screen TV. They are vital to the production of hybrid and electric vehicles, medical imaging equipment, advanced magnets, and a range of other technologies. These examples should demonstrate that many of the niceties and necessities we enjoy are possible thanks to rare earth elements, which we must have in large quantities.

There's a science to elements many in the media miss. First, there are seventeen rare earth elements, each of which has its own special applications: *cerium, dysprosium, erbium, europium, gadolinium, holmium, lanthanum, lutetium, neodymium, praseodymium, promethium, samarium, scandium, terbium, thulium, ytterbium, and yttrium.*

Rare Earth Elements Applications

- **Scandium is found in everything from flat-screen televisions to baseball bats, bike frames, and fishing rods.**
- **Yttrium produces phosphors that are widely used in cell phones. It's also used in camera lenses and is relied on for solar-panel batteries.**
- **Neodymium can be found in tanning beds and light bulbs, and its mixture with other more common metals creates neodymium magnets found in lifesaving medical equipment like MRI machines.**

Second, the phrase "rare earth elements" is a misnomer. Most of these elements aren't particularly rare. For instance, cerium is the twenty-fifth most common element in the earth's crust. There's more cerium within our planet than there is copper.

What the *rare* in rare earth element refers to is how these elements are discovered in usable quantities. Unlike more common metals like copper or more precious metals like silver and gold, rare earth metals are not typically found in rich veins that can be mined by the ton over the course of many years. These metals are instead uncovered scattered in smaller pockets, often in hard-to-reach places, like six miles down at the bottom of the ocean.

Most people assume that these vital elements are found for the most part in and around China. Roughly 80 percent of America's supply of these special metals comes from there. It's understandable why, for several decades, most Americans haven't thought twice about all our critical electronics components coming from a hostile communist country. After all, everything else—from the junk we buy in Walmart to the active ingredients in our medicine—does. China took over the worldwide market for rare earth elements the same way it cornered most markets: by blunt force. For years, the Chinese communist regime was perfectly happy using the most environmentally damaging mining techniques to maximize profits while paying no regard to the havoc it was inflicting on its country's ecosystems. The newsmagazine *60 Minutes* investigated the rare earth elements industry and it's a bit shocking what they found: "video from a freelance cameraman showing the area near Baotou, China's rare earth capital, where the air, land, and water are so saturated with chemical toxins, the Chinese have had to relocate entire villages."

Do you think the Chinese government ever shut down a mining operation because it might damage the habitat of a spotted newt or some other species no one has ever heard of? We're talking about the same Chinese government that has, for years, openly run concentration camps for Muslim ethnic minorities where rape is rampant, as are forced abortions, sterilization, and an untold number of other human rights atrocities that occur on a daily basis. China also flooded the rare earth metal market to push other countries out of it. They did the same thing to the smelting industry in America with cheap copper and other metals used in industry. If you're reading this book, you're likely aware of the fact that it's simply immoral that China's communist regime controls 80 percent of the market for elements critical to our national defense, technology, and medical industries. What you may not know is that this danger isn't merely theoretical. That's because China hasn't hesitated to wield its rare earth elements monopoly as a weapon against other countries.

In 2010, China shut down exports of rare earth elements to Japan over a political dispute. Japan had arrested the captain of a Chinese fishing vessel after he was caught fishing in Japanese waters. It's the kind of geopolitical spat that occurs somewhere in the world almost every day. But China turned it into economic warfare by attempting to bring Japan's electronics industry to its knees. Even if you don't know anything else about Japan, you know that *everything* there is electronic. This set off a series of export restrictions by China not only to Japan, but to other destinations, including the United States. After the United States joined other nations in opening a case with the World Trade Organization (WTO) accusing the communist country of breaking trade agreements, Chinese government officials told the WTO that the changes were made to protect the environment. If you believe that, I've got a bridge in Brooklyn that I'd like to sell you!

If China has weaponized its mining industry once, why would anyone reasonably argue that they won't do it again? Despite common sense, some people will. And that probably means they're on China's payroll. The prudent recognize that it is in America's best interest to not remain beholden to China for these vital elements.

The fact is, if the trade war President Trump launched against China got really hot, the regime would attempt to cripple the United States by shutting off the supply of rare earth elements we so desperately depend on. Luckily, the Trump White House has recognized this vulnerability. Peter Navarro, the director of the Office of Trade and Manufacturing Policy (OTMP), considers this an important problem to solve. In a letter published on FloridaPolitics.com, Navarro wrote:

> **Indeed, prior administration's failures to combat China's economic aggression created a strategic risk in the productions and availability of rare earth elements: "China's domination of the rare earth element market ... illustrates the potentially dangerous interaction between Chinese economic aggression guided by its strategic industrial policies and vulnerabilities and gaps in America's manufacturing and defense industrial base. China has strategically flooded the global market with rare earths at subsidized prices, driven out competitors and deterred new market entrants. When China needs to flex its soft power muscles by embargoing rare earths, it does not hesitate."**

We must not allow this aggressive behavior by the Chinese to cause the same risks to strategic or indispensable materials.

Either we take steps to ensure that America is able to identify, develop, and utilize its numerous natural resources, including strategic materials such as copper, molybdenum and silver, or we cede control of our national defense and economic security to unstable countries or strategic adversaries.

It's certainly a ray of sunshine to know that the smartest people in the Trump administration are addressing a vulnerability for the country that's been exploited by our mortal enemies for decades. What can be done? On one hand, America can increase imports from friendly noncommunist nations. Australia has rare earth elements, as do quite a few other places, like Estonia, which produces 2 percent of the rare earth elements. But the long-game solution to our rare earth elements problem is to mine them in this country—which is happening for the first time since the Manhattan Project began during World War II.

In 2018, President Trump ordered the Pentagon to find alternate sources of rare earth elements for use in sensitive defense projects. This has led directly to the Army funding the development of rare earth element mining and refining, the first investment of its kind since the 1940s. It's a good start. There is still a lot of work to be done to bring America up to speed in the race to procure these precious metals. They may not be precious in the traditional sense of gold and silver but they are even more precious in the electronic era.

It turns out that the most abundant source of rare earth elements may be the ocean floor. The Pacific Ocean in particular has huge fields of these metals in the form of black spheres called nodules. Dozens of countries including China, Russia, and even Canada are racing to figure out how to scoop these nodules out of the ocean. But America is still sitting on the sidelines. We're talking about minerals worth at least $16 *trillion*, which you'd think would be enough to get Uncle Sam off his ass. Maybe now that America is back in the rare earth elements business domestically, our leaders will be willing to go into the deep, dark depths of the ocean to free us once and for all from dependence on China for the lifeblood of an already booming tech economy.

31.

THE TRUMP ADMINISTRATION STRUCK A $1 BILLION DEAL TO PROVIDE HIV PREVENTION DRUGS FREE TO 200,000 UNINSURED AMERICANS EVERY YEAR FOR THE NEXT DECADE

In February 2019, President Trump unveiled an ambitious plan to eradicate the transmission of HIV within a decade. "Together, we will defeat AIDS in America and beyond," the president declared of the pandemic disease that has caused an estimated 32 million deaths worldwide between 1981 and 2018. "In recent years we have made remarkable progress in the fight against HIV and AIDS. Scientific breakthroughs have brought a once-distant dream within reach," Trump told the nation in his State of the Union address. "My budget will ask Democrats and Republicans to make the needed commitment to eliminate the HIV epidemic in the United States within 10 years. Together, we will defeat AIDS in America."

An estimated 1.1 million Americans had HIV in 2019. Another

40,000 Americans are diagnosed every year. Health and Human Services (HHS) projects that some 400,000 Americans will contract the deadly virus over the next decade. The direct annual taxpayer cost for HIV prevention alone figures at $20 billion. The government fears that figure could climb as injection drug use continues to soar. "One in 10 new HIV infections occurs among people who inject drugs," the Centers for Disease Control and Prevention (CDC) says.

The president proposed, and Congress approved and appropriated in its 2020 fiscal budget, a historic $291 million to fund the first phase of the administration's bold plan to end HIV. The administration's initiative, known as Ending the HIV Epidemic: A Plan for America (EHE), seeks to reduce new U.S. HIV infections by 75 percent over the next five years and by 90 percent by 2030. By May 2019, Health and Human Services Secretary Alex Azar II had rolled out a new program, Ready, Set, PrEP. Azar also announced that his agency had secured a donation of drugs, worth billions, from Gilead Sciences that would see the pharmaceutical company donate pre-exposure prophylaxis (PrEP) medication for up to 200,000 individuals each year for up to 11 years. A 30-day supply of the HIV prevention drug can carry a $2,000 price tag for people without insurance, HHS says. Program participants are individuals without prescription drug coverage who have tested negative for HIV and have a valid on-label prescription for PrEP.

Studies have shown that PrEP reduces the risk of getting HIV from sex by about 99 percent when taken consistently. Among people who inject drugs,

> PrEP reduces the risk of getting HIV by at least 74
> percent when taken consistently.
> —Centers for Disease Control and Prevention

The CDC estimates that in 2018 roughly 220,000 individuals had received a prescription for PrEP, which the agency says reduces the chances of contracting HIV through sex by up to 97 percent. Coverage, though, comes with a stark racial divide, the CDC claims. Coverage was particularly low among those groups who contract HIV at a disproportionately high rate: young gay and bisexual people and minorities, according to the agency. White Americans were estimated to be between four and seven times more likely to be covered for PrEP than their black and Latino counterparts, CDC data showed.

While black Americans represent only 13 percent of the overall population, they accounted for 42 percent of new HIV diagnoses in 2018, according to CDC data. One in two gay black men in America will be diagnosed with HIV over the course of their lifetime, the CDC warned in 2016. The agency notes that one in four gay and bisexual Hispanic men and one in every eleven gay and bisexual white men are at risk of contracting the deadly HIV virus, which causes AIDS, over the course of their life. The number of new cases of black women with HIV has dropped by 40 percent in recent years, the agency said, but infection rates have seen a sharp increase among young gay men, especially blacks. "Blacks account for more new HIV infections, people estimated to be living with HIV disease, and HIV-related deaths than any other racial-ethnic group in the U.S," the Kaiser Family Foundation commented.

President Trump's HIV eradication plan poses promise, particularly after New York City saw a record reduction in HIV infections in 2018, thanks in large part to PrEP. Mayor Bill de Blasio enacted the NYC Ending the Epidemic Plan in 2015. The three-part plan focused on identifying, tracking, and treating city residents with HIV. The city that was once the epicenter of America's AIDS crisis has provided a blueprint for the federal government's vision to end the epidemic.

Enlisting agencies like the CDC and the National Institutes of Health for the first five years, the Trump administration plans that the first phase will see these various agencies concentrate their attention in HIV hotspots around the nation, including those in southern and northern Florida, southern California, Seattle, Washington, Texas, and Atlanta, where infection rates are consistently high. "More than 50 percent of new HIV diagnoses in 2016 and 2017 occurred in 48 counties, Washington, DC, and San Juan, Puerto Rico," the CDC said. Honing in on Alabama, Arkansas, Kentucky, Mississippi, Missouri, Oklahoma, and South Carolina, which have an elevated occurrence of HIV, the government will bombard these regions with information campaigns, new diagnostic resources, and increased investments in treatment programs.

By March 2020, access to HIV PrEP medications was available to qualifying participants at CVS Health, Walgreens, and Rite Aid locations. The three companies, with a combined total of more than 21,000 locations, donated their dispensing services to HHS as part of the national program to prevent the spread of HIV.

32.

TRUMP USHERED IN A LANDMARK TRADE PACT TO REPLACE THE NORTH AMERICAN FREE TRADE AGREEMENT THAT COST THE U.S. MILLIONS OF JOBS

The U.S. Bureau of Labor Statistics revealed in 2018 that nearly 4.5 million manufacturing jobs have been lost overall since the North American Free Trade Agreement (NAFTA) took effect in 1994. Of course, technology, automation, and state-to-state competition were among the many factors that all played a role over the near–quarter-century that saw these jobs vanish. Still, the U.S. trade deficit with Mexico and Canada under NAFTA eliminated an estimated one million net jobs in the United States by 2004, the Economic Policy Institute (EPI) estimates. That gutting of the U.S. job market doesn't include the job loss due to China's becoming a member of the World Trade Organization in 2000, which precipitated the loss of roughly five million U.S. jobs from 2000 to 2014. So, it's no surprise that Trump slipped on the brass knuckles when one of the crowning achievements of his presidency, a sweeping multinational trade deal to replace NAFTA, was being stalled by Canada.

One of the great or headline-making and headache-inducing things about Donald Trump is his ability to not mince words and leave audiences guessing. He certainly isn't shy about telling world leaders when he strongly disagrees with their policies, even if it throws diplomats into a tizzy. That's precisely why Trump won what experts called a long-shot election in 2016. And one of Trump's favorite targets is close to home: Canada's Prime Minister Justin Trudeau.

One of the things Trump and Trudeau clashed on is the United States-Mexico–Canada Agreement (USMCA). The pact officially replaced NAFTA when the Canadian Parliament ratified the USMCA in March 2020. But Trudeau loved NAFTA, and for good reason. NAFTA, established in January 1994, was a tremendous boon for both Canada and Mexico, creating $100 billion in trade deficits of products shipped between both countries and the United States.

Trump didn't hold anything back in explaining how much he hated NAFTA. He derided the Clinton-era trade deal as a "disaster" and went so far as to call it "the worst trade deal maybe ever signed anywhere." Trump didn't hesitate to take his war on NAFTA to Twitter, with a constant drumbeat of tweets like this one: "We were far better off before NAFTA—should never have been signed. Even the Vat Tax was not accounted for. We make new deal or go back to pre-NAFTA!" One of Trump's most searing criticisms of NAFTA focused on Canada, whom Trump accused of "decades of abuse" of America under the trade agreement. If you really dig into some of Canada's actions, you'll find that Trump has a strong case.

NAFTA put the emphasis on the *FT* portion of the name, free trade. Both Canada and Mexico enjoyed the fruits of free trade with

America but fell back into trade practices about as free as North Korea when it came to protecting their own industries.

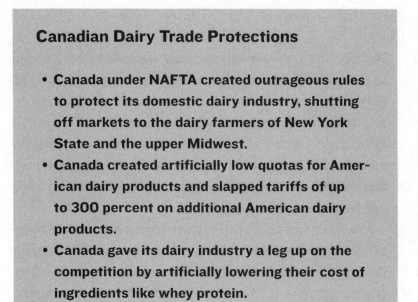

Canadian Dairy Trade Protections

- Canada under **NAFTA** created outrageous rules to protect its domestic dairy industry, shutting off markets to the dairy farmers of New York State and the upper Midwest.
- Canada created artificially low quotas for American dairy products and slapped tariffs of up to 300 percent on additional American dairy products.
- Canada gave its dairy industry a leg up on the competition by artificially lowering their cost of ingredients like whey protein.

How exactly is that free trade? That's exactly the question and quagmire that vexed American industry long before Trump took office. The dairy industry was particularly bludgeoned by Canada's so-called free trade rules, but it was far from the only sector of the American economy that was impacted. Phil Kerpen, the president of American Commitment, an organization dedicated to limited government and economic growth, explained some of Canada's abuses in an op-ed for the *Washington Post*. Kerpen wrote that Canada has emerged as an abuser of intellectual property (IP) rights.

As IP has become a more critical component of the global economy, Canada has begun to play fast and loose with America's economy. One way that Canada has ripped off America is by enabling counterfeit Chinese goods to flow across its border.

> **But Canada's sudden appearance alongside China on the list of the worst IP abusers is more of a surprise. The report finds that "significant concerns include poor border and law enforcement with respect to counterfeit or pirated goods, weak patent and pricing environment for innovative pharmaceuticals, deficient copyright protection, and inadequate transparency and due process regarding geographical indications."**
>
> **In other words, Canada is not letting our customs officials stop pirated and counterfeit goods that flow through Canada into the United States. Nor are the Canadians enforcing the laws themselves—they conducted exactly zero criminal prosecutions for counterfeiting in 2017. Thus they have been serving as an enabler to Chinese companies and other high-volume counterfeiters.**

Kerpen also believes that Canada's poorly defined "educational exception" on copyright allows Canadians to use material created by Americans without paying the piper. Under Trump, the United States would no longer accept free trade when it benefited our neighbors to the north and south, but didn't help America. It's a consistent theme of his presidency. The USMCA provides a remedy: It establishes a Committee on Intellectual Property Rights, with the express purpose of enforcing IP rights and preventing the theft of trade secrets. The pact also extends the terms of copyright to seventy years beyond the life of the author. That's up from fifty years in NAFTA.

The road to ratification of the USMCA was a rocky one. In fact, Trump smacked Canada in 2018 with a punitive tariff on steel and aluminum. Canada quickly learned a bitter lesson. It wasn't the only country in a "free trade" agreement that could apply protectionist tariffs on its trading partners. Trudeau was adamant that he wouldn't be pushed around by America. In fact, the tariffs were in place for just about a year until both Canada and Mexico became more agreeable to ratifying the USMCA. Canada's and Mexico's political leaders had agreed to the terms of the trade deal in September 2018. The U.S. Congress supported the deal, which still faced over a year of behind-the-scenes negotiations between congressional Democrats and the Trump administration. The U.S. overwhelmingly approved USMCA in December 2019. The Senate passed it a month later. "I will say that we just ended a nightmare known as NAFTA," President Trump told a packed plant of autoworkers in Warren, Michigan, one day after signing the three-country trade deal into law. After months of political wrangling, the Canadian Parliament finally ratified the USMCA in March 2020.

U.S. Trade Representative Robert Lighthizer said, "Now that the USMCA has been approved by all three countries, a historic new chapter for North American trade has begun." But for Donald Trump, this was just another win for American workers and another loss for countries wishing to continue treating the United States and its citizens like an ATM.

33.

PRESIDENT TRUMP'S TRADE WAR WITH CHINA IS SUPPORTED BY 80 PERCENT OF FARMERS

Donald Trump highlighted the hazard of two major issues that have long been ignored by America's political establishment: immigration and trade. The president promised to crack down on illegal immigration and enact a merit-based immigration system. He also vowed to replace one-sided trade deals such as NAFTA and to target China's unfair trade practices—policies that have been particularly crushing for American farmers. Trump launched his tariff war with China in the summer of 2018 and farmers have backed the aggressive effort, despite the elite media's attempt to drive a wedge between them and the president.

What began as an outlier quickly coalesced into an irrefutable statistical consensus: a majority of America's farmers overwhelmingly support President Trump taking the fight to China on trade.

U.S. Farmers Support President Trump

Agri-Pulse, an industry publication, released a survey in November 2018 that found that, of 600 commercial farmers, 79 percent backed President Trump's increased aggression toward China's communist regime. The poll represented an equal number of small, medium, and large farms. Further, farmers who identify as Republican strongly backed Trump's tariff fight with China. Ninety-two percent of Republican farmers approved of the way Trump is handling his presidency, while 33 percent of Democrats and 65 percent of independent farmers disapprove of Trump's handling of his first term in office. "When asked which political party relates to you and your farming interests, 65 percent said it was the GOP compared to only 9 percent who selected Democrats," *Agri-Pulse* concluded.

Elsewhere, a Farm Journal Pulse poll conducted in July 2019 revealed that 79 percent of farmers approve of the president's job, which was up from 74 percent in June 2019. Fifty-three percent said that they "strongly approve" of President Trump, up from 50 percent in June of that year. A Purdue Center for Commercial Agriculture survey released in August 2019 found that the center's overall expectations index rose to 159, which was the highest rating in two years. **That month, a** *New York Times* **headline screamed, "Farmers' Frustration with Trump Grows as U.S. Escalates China Fight." This 1,900-word article was published amid an avalanche of polling that pointed to a completely different reality: Most of America's farmers back the president's fight for fairer trade policies with China. And the longer the president pursued his pressure campaign against the communist country, the more the** *New York Times* **reporting fell out of alignment with political reality. A Farm Journal Pulse survey released in October 2019 also found that three-quarters of farmers approved of the president, up five points from August.**

There were about 2.6 million farmers working in 2018, according to the U.S. Department of Agriculture. That figure represented about 1.3 percent of the U.S. labor force. It's not a large voting bloc, but that's never proved to be part of President Trump's motivation for freeing farmers from the crushing trade practices pushed by China. President Trump vowed to help those farmers suffering from years of China's retaliatory tariffs with federal money collected by the tariffs the U.S. government imposed on the communist country. "Our deal with China, our deal with so many—they're all coming along very, very nicely," Trump said in October 2019, a month before he bypassed Congress to send some $20 billion in aid to farmers and corporate agricultural enterprises. "Our farmers, by the way, have been incredible. They've been incredible."

Farmers also publicly supported the president's actions to open the Chinese markets for American products. "At this point, we've gone this far, we want to make sure we get a good deal," said Iowa farmer Grant Kimberly, who is also the director of market development at the Iowa Soybean Association, in December 2019. Farmers' support for President Trump rose to a record high in January 2020, according to a Farm Journal Pulse survey, which featured responses from 1,286 farmers, and found that 83 percent supported President Trump. In contrast, only 16 percent disapproved of the president.

"Of note is the strongly approve category went up three percentage points from an already lofty December number and his higher overall approval ratings ever," said Jim Wiesemeyer, a Pro Farmer policy analyst. "That says the president's approval is rock-solid. With the recent upbeat news on USMCA and the Phase 1 accord with China, the ratings will likely remain firm ahead." The share of farmers who stated that they "strongly approve" of the president rose to 64 percent, or nearly two-thirds, up from 61 percent at the end of 2019. Only 19 percent of farmers said that they "somewhat approve" of the president's performance, while three percent said that they "somewhat disapprove." Wiesemeyer noted that the rural farming vote counts as an integral part of President Trump's electoral coalition.

"Trump needs the rural vote to keep the same states he won in 2016 in his win column come November," Wiesemeyer said. "In fact, contacts say he is focusing on winning Minnesota this time as a backstop should he lose a state he won in 2016. That means agriculture will continue to be a key topic in the president's re-election campaign."

President Trump's advocacy for the American farmer has also garnered him electoral support among Iowans. A March 2020 *Des Moines Register*/Mediacom survey found that Trump led former vice president Joe Biden and Senator Bernie Sanders (I-VT) by double digits in a hypothetical election matchup. Independent voter Steve Jorgensen told the *Des Moines Register* that the president's support for farmers had increased Iowans' support for the forty-fifth president. "There are some things about the man, personally, I don't care for, but policy, yes," Jorgensen said of President Trump. "His trade policies—particularly for the farmers—I think in the long run, are going to turn out great. A lot of us right now are kind of in-between. It's tough out here, buddy. But it's coming around."

Glen Brunkow, a Kansas farmer who grows soybeans and corn and raises sheep and cattle, voted for Trump and plans on voting for the president again in 2020. "At this point, I would say it looks like it," Brunkow told Yahoo Finance in February 2020. "It depends on the candidate, and it depends on their stance on issues as they relate to [agriculture], and any of the other topics that are hot button issues to me. As I look at the field now, he probably aligns the best."

Brunkow added that farmers are particularly sensitive to additional taxes and that the president's rollback of the inheritance tax, often referred to as the "death tax," greatly helped them. "I don't want to see any more taxes—whether it's an increase in the income tax [or] increase in sales tax," he added. "The inheritance tax, having that rolled back was a great benefit to us in agriculture. We don't intend to sell our land when changing generations. . . . We're running our razors in margin, so any increase in taxes really hurts us."

"If [Trump] came out in favor of a big tax increase, more regulations, or cut back in trade, any of those things," Brunkow said when asked what would potentially change his mind. "You really need to know who the other candidate is. In looking at the Democratic field, it doesn't look like there's any [appealing candidates] at initial first blush." Brunkow added that he does not see any particular Democratic candidate who appeals to him, and that includes presumptive front-runner former vice president Joe Biden.

34.

TRUMP SAVED THOUSANDS OF APPLE JOBS IN TEXAS FROM BEING SHIPPED TO CHINA MONTHS BEFORE THE CORONAVIRUS PANDEMIC BEGAN THERE

Roughly four months before the coronavirus pandemic plunged the whole planet into a health and economic crisis, Apple was set to move its Mac Pro production from Austin, Texas, to Shanghai, China, a city just a two-hour plane ride east of Wuhan, where the deadly virus first emerged. The move would allow Apple to avoid incurring the cost of nearly all its imports from China as the Trump administration was threatening to levy tariffs against the communist regime.

It's no secret that President Trump has a contentious relationship with the Silicon Valley Masters of the Universe. The leftist leadership of giant tech companies like Google and Facebook despise the president and the America First movement that swept him into office. Despite the dramatic political differences, Trump has forged a working relationship with one superpowered tech CEO, Tim Cook, or "Tim Apple" as the president has called him. Apple is different from most of the tech giants that rule the Internet. While Google and Facebook suck up every scrap of information about your private life to sell to the highest bidder, Apple touts its willingness to keep your personal information confidential in TV ad campaigns. Apple is simply more interested in selling expensive devices and the software that runs on them. Tim Cook has made his shareholders a fortune with Apple's carefully styled and extremely reliable gadgets, ranging from iPhones to MacBooks. The company that Steve Jobs built has become the ultimate marketing machine. Do you even *know* someone under the age of twenty-one who doesn't own AirPods?

It also helps that Tim Cook speaks Trump's language—the language of traditional business and marketing. But it hasn't always been a rosy relationship, described by the press as a "bromance." In 2019, Apple felt the heat of a textbook Trump thrashing. Most of Apple's products are built in China. The company's image has taken his lashings in recent years as the general public has come to learn about the manufacturing practices involved in putting together their devices. For example, news of Apple's iPhone manufacturing partner Foxconn installing suicide nets under the upper windows of its factory to prevent employees from killing themselves in between shifts generated hundreds of international news headlines and thousands of social media memes.

Although most of Apple's expensive merchandise comes from China, one of the company's iconic products is made here in the United States. Apple assembles its Mac Pro desktops in Austin, Texas, and has since 2013. Mac Pros are not your average desktop computer. We're talking about supercomputers coveted by sophisticated graphics pros with a price tag that typically starts at $6,000.

You can get your whole family iPhones and AirPods for that kind of money!

As America's trade war with China started to heat up in 2019, startling news came out of Apple's Silicon Valley headquarters. The *Wall Street Journal* reported that Tim Cook planned to move production of the powerful Mac Pro desktops out of Texas and into communist China. Trump world and even some experts on China were taken aback by Apple's purported move. China expert Gordon Chang commented on the surprise move to Breitbart News editor in chief Alex Marlow on SiriusXM's *Breitbart News Daily*. Chang didn't mince words, calling Cook's decision "unbelievable." According to Chang, "Apple has told us which side it's on. I'm just at a loss for words at what Apple is doing by moving production of the Mac Pro out of Austin, Texas, to Shanghai."

Chang may have been left at a loss for words but that's never been something that could be said of Donald Trump. One of America's richest companies shipping good-paying jobs overseas goes to the core of President Trump's America First ethos. The president promised to make Apple feel the pain of its decision to move the Texas plant. Trump knew the weak point of Cook's plan was that he didn't intend to make China the major market for those high-dollar Mac Pros. Apple planned to ship their supercomputers to the United States. And that fact gave Trump his biggest bargaining chip: potential tariffs on Apple products, which would hit Apple— and its shareholders—financially.

"Apple will not be given Tariff waiver, or relief, for Mac Pro parts that are made in China. Make them in the USA, no Tariffs!" the president said in one fiery tweet. No bluster. No personal attacks.

Trump simply promised to bite a big chunk out of Apple's desktop profits through tariffs on Chinese manufacturing. Mere days after Trump issued his threat, Apple changed its tune. During its quarterly earnings call, Cook said, "We've been making the Mac Pro in the United States. We want to continue doing that. We're working and investing currently in the capacity to do so. We want to continue to be there."

At the same time as Cook's earnings call, Trump was using a much kinder tone with reporters. "A man I have a lot of liking for and respect is Tim Cook, and we'll work it out, I think they're going to announce that they're going to build a plant in Texas, and if they do that I'm starting to get very happy," Trump said. Several months after the exchange, Trump and Cook visited the Austin facility together. There, the president underscored his earlier message, saying, "When you build in the United States, you don't have to worry about tariffs. It sort of helps people make a decision to come in."

In November 2019, Apple broke ground on the new $1 billion campus in the sterling southern city, which would house 5,000 Apple jobs for Texans. The eventual head count could reach as high as 15,000 workers. It was Donald Trump who swung into action for the city of Austin and the Texans working in the tech sector for Apple when Tim Cook wanted to ship their jobs overseas. And Apple should be thanking Trump for fighting to keep Mac Pro production in the United States as the coronavirus has decimated China's high-tech manufacturing economy and several of its supply chains.

35.

THE TRUMP TAX CUTS BROUGHT $1 TRILLION IN CORPORATE PROFITS TO THE U.S. FROM OVERSEAS

You know, there are days that I think being the black entertainment editor of the world's most prominent conservative news organization is a stressful job. Then I think about what it must feel like to be an international tax accountant. That's when I thank my lucky stars that I only have to deal with the entire mainstream media hating my guts.

American companies do business around the world. This is nothing new. You can go to every corner of the world and find Apple products for sale, although I don't think there is an Apple store in Antarctica yet. But if there was, the company would find a way to avoid paying U.S. taxes on its profits. For decades, avoiding U.S. taxes has been treated as a fact of life for big businesses.

The argument here isn't that all overseas profits are bad. If you're Chevron, you need to keep some profits outside the United States because you need to fund your far-flung operations and acquire assets to expand your business. That's not what President Trump was focusing on at all when he began calling attention to the need to repatriate overseas profits. Trump's focus was on so-called overseas cash stashes. Companies like Apple, Microsoft, and practically every other major multinational corporation, especially tech companies, pile up huge amounts of cash in overseas tax havens, like Ireland, instead of bringing the money home and paying U.S. tax rates on it. Apple led the pack with about $250 billion stashed in Ireland. Were they keeping it for a rainy day? Not likely. Stashing profits overseas comes with significant downsides for companies. For example, they can't use the funds for a stock buyback, which increases shareholder value.

The upside of keeping profits offshore was just too high for America's biggest companies. The motivation for keeping profits overseas was to avoid paying the punishing 35 percent corporate tax, established in 1993. Major companies saw that U.S. corporate tax rate, among the highest in the world, as simply too much to bear so they worked hard to keep the profits away from U.S. shores. Think about how hard the average citizen works to avoid paying taxes. Is your couch counted as a home office on your tax return? A trip to Chuck E. Cheese is a business expense? If you make the stakes billions instead of thousands, you end up with complicated corporate tax tricks designed to keep Uncle Sam's hand out of giant corporations' pockets.

The gory details of how corporations dodged U.S. corporate taxes would bore you to tears, but it is worth noting. Take, for example, Apple. It's both one of the world's most profitable companies and a homegrown success story. A nerdy computer whiz and a marketing genius started creating computers in a garage and went on to become the trendsetter for consumer electronics. Apple is a worldwide economic phenomenon. It's also the most creative player in the overseas profits shell game. The California company pioneered the "double Irish flip," an infamous tax arrangement designed to move profits around to reflect the least amount of taxability—if there is any tax paid at all. Apple got more creative from there. My personal favorite is an arrangement called the "double Irish with a Dutch sandwich." Honestly, these sound less like tax avoidance schemes and more like X Games skateboard tricks. Why does Ireland keep coming up? Apple and other Silicon Valley companies were pretty much able to rewrite the country's tax code, effectively turning it into tax haven heaven, kind of like how the Obama administration let Silicon Valley create net neutrality for its own benefit.

Apple's tax tricks in Ireland would make a career criminal blush. The U.S. Senate Permanent Subcommittee on Investigations revealed that in 2011 Apple's Ireland subsidiary paid taxes of $10 million on profits of $22 billion. I'll save you from doing the math. That's a tax rate of 0.05 percent. By the way, all the profits from this book will be funneled through my Irish subsidiary, Jerome O'Hudson.

As I mentioned earlier, Apple piled up about $250 billion in Ireland. That number may not mean much to you; it's basically Monopoly money for you and me. But to put that in perspective, Howard Silverblatt, senior index analyst at S&P Dow Jones Indices, explained that, on its own, Apple's cash pile would be in the top 20 of the S&P 500. Amazing, isn't it? And it was sitting offshore instead of being pumped back into the American economy.

In comes President Trump. A pragmatic problem solver, he approached the dilemma of American companies hiding huge profits overseas like a simple math equation. A businessman himself, Trump understood that the crux of the problem was in the tax rate. I'm sure he's used some creative tax tricks in his heyday. If he didn't, the man has worked for years in show business, home of the infamous studio profit-making method known as "Hollywood accounting."

Trump and his economic team set an audacious goal. They wanted to bring home the untold wealth that rightfully belonged in the United States. President Trump explained, "By making it less punitive for companies to bring back this money, and by making the process far less bureaucratic and difficult, we can return trillions and trillions of dollars to our economy and spur billions of dollars in new investments in our struggling communities throughout our nation."

Bringing corporate profits back to America killed several birds with one stone. First, the federal Leviathan could quench its thirst with the flood of new tax revenues. Additionally, companies would be free to use the money however they pleased, and, inevitably, it would benefit Americans in myriad ways. Some would argue that the companies would just sit on the money in America as they did in Ireland and elsewhere, but that really wouldn't be an option. These public companies would face a revolt from their shareholders if they didn't actively invest their profits and build shareholder value. "Investment by the top 15 cash holders also rose in 2018, particularly relative to other nonfinancial S&P 500 firms. For the top 15 cash holders, the average ratio of investment (capital expenditures plus research and development expenses) to assets rose from 2.3 percent in 2017 to 2.8 percent in 2018, while it remained flat at 1.5 percent for other nonfinancial S&P 500 firms," according to research from the Board of Governors of the Federal Reserve System. The Federal Reserve investigated how the Tax Cuts and Jobs Act of 2017 affected corporations' decisions to invest after the law was passed. The Federal Reserve noted that "investment by the top 15 cash holders was already on an upward trajectory for several years prior to the TCJA—both in dollar terms . . . and relative to other nonfinancial S&P 500 firms."

Trump's plan swung into action as part of his sweeping 2017 tax cuts. Most Americans likely reacted to the passage of the Tax Cuts and Jobs Act of 2017 as Trump changing our taxes for the better.

While that's true, the reform made bringing money home extremely attractive to giant corporations like Apple and General Electric, among others. The Trump tax overhaul lowered the corporate rate from 35 percent to a one-time 15.5 percent on cash and 8 percent on non-cash or illiquid assets like factory equipment. The plan also made taxes on the cash stashes payable over eight years, another term attractive to both the corporations and government coffers, which would get a boost each year instead of one giant jolt.

> Apple announced in 2018 that it would "spend $350 billion on development and create 20,000 jobs in the United States in the next five years," according to the *Washington Post*. Trump responded to the news with congratulations. "I promised that my policies would allow companies like Apple to bring massive amounts of money back to the United States. Great to see Apple follow through as a result of TAX CUTS. Huge win for American workers and the USA!"

Over the course of 2018 and 2019, U.S. companies brought $1 trillion dollars back into the American economy from their tax havens overseas as a result of the historic tax cuts law. Trump leveraged his business experience to solve a problem that previous administrations ignored—or didn't have a prayer of passing—creating a solution that benefited shareholders and taxpayers, and even earned the grudging respect of the CEOs of America's biggest companies.

36.

FEDERAL EMPLOYEE PAY INCREASED 3 PERCENT IN 2020, A DECADE HIGH, AND MILLIONS NOW BENEFIT FROM TWELVE-WEEK PAID PARENTAL LEAVE

Donald Trump has an uncanny knack for co-opting political issues that Democrats have dominated for decades (think trade). With the passage of paid family leave for federal workers, Congress is free to promote measures that make it easier for Americans to start families, while avoiding legislation that would create new government bureaucracies or hike taxes.

In December 2019, President Trump signed a $1.4 trillion spending bill that set the stage for a conservative movement for paid family leave. The spending bill repealed some parts of the Affordable Care Act (ACA), or Obamacare, included tax cuts, and, among other things, increased pay for civilian federal employees by 3.1 percent starting in 2020. This signifies the most substantial pay raise for federal employees, including members of the military, in a decade. Before signing the bill, the president portrayed the pay increase as a

Christmas gift to America's military. "As we head into Christmas, I am proud to report that we are giving every soldier, sailor, airman, Coast Guardsman, and Marine a well-earned pay raise. In January, each of you will see the largest increase that you have had in such a long time," Trump said in December 2019.

The defense spending bill also repealed the widow's tax, which allowed widows and widowers to qualify for survivor benefits from only one program, even if they qualified for several different programs under the Department of Defense (DOD) and the Department of Veterans Affairs (VA). This means that every dollar received in benefit would be taken away from other widows and widowers. "The tax is gone," Trump said. "That was very important to us. The 'widow's tax' is gone."

The bill also extended federal civilian employees' parental leave to three months after the birth or adoption of a child. President Trump said at the time that granting paid leave to federal workers will fulfill promises to the government's workforce.

The spending bill's advancement of paid family leave for federal employees sets the stage for Congress to pass a paid family leave bill for all Americans. President Donald Trump has championed paid family leave as a way to expand benefits for the American family, which is typically a conservative position. But Democrats have long owned the issue of family leave, going back to the Bill Clinton-era Family Medical Leave Act (FMLA). The FMLA allows Americans to take time off after the birth or adoption of a child. However, there is no provision in the law for families to receive a salary while they take time off to care for the newborn. The FMLA ensures that parents can obtain twelve weeks of unpaid leave without the fear of losing their job; however, some parents cannot afford to lose three months' income.

In 2016, half of those working Americans who took leave used savings set aside for something else to cover lost wages due to child-care expenses. Another 37 percent took on debt, and 41 percent cut their leave time short.

A Rutgers University study found that women who have access to paid family leave are 39 percent less likely to obtain welfare and 40 percent less likely to seek out food stamps in the year following their child's birth when compared to those who do not have paid leave.

Several studies also show that the availability of paid family leave boosts worker morale, increases company productivity, and reduces employee turnover. An Independent Women's Forum (IWF) poll released in May 2019 found that 73 percent of Americans, 60 percent of Republicans, 72 percent of Independents, and 83 percent of Democrats back a paid family leave proposal. "Americans want a paid leave approach that threads the needle: providing support for parents who need it, but without unfairly shifting costs to others, growing government, or discouraging employers from providing benefits on their own," IWF president Carrie Lukas said.

Americans across the political spectrum widely agree that parents should have flexibility with the paid leave benefit and that a paid leave program should not increase the national deficit.

During his State of the Union address in February 2020, President Trump called on Congress to pass a bipartisan paid family leave bill. Trump urged Congress to pass the Advancing Support for Working Families Act, which would give "family leave to mothers and fathers all across the Nation."

"Forty million American families have an average $2,200 extra thanks to our child tax credit," Trump said. "And I sent the Congress

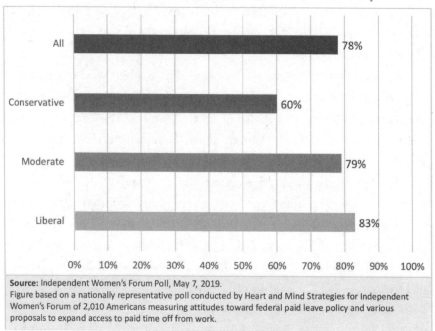

Americans' Desire for Federal Paid Leave Policy

All	78%
Conservative	60%
Moderate	79%
Liberal	83%

Source: Independent Women's Forum Poll, May 7, 2019.
Figure based on a nationally representative poll conducted by Heart and Mind Strategies for Independent Women's Forum of 2,010 Americans measuring attitudes toward federal paid leave policy and various proposals to expand access to paid time off from work.

a plan with a vision to further expand access to high-quality child-care and urge you to act immediately," he added.

Indeed, Trump and Republican lawmakers can lead on paid family leave. The United States is the only industrialized country without access to paid family leave and suffers the highest infant mortality rate among industrialized nations.

Senator Bill Cassidy (R-LA) has been working with Senator Kyrsten Sinema (D-AZ) to craft the Advancing Support for Working Families Act, which would serve as the bill that Cassidy believes could pass through Congress with bipartisan support. This bill would allow parents to receive a $5,000 paid leave benefit advance

Americans' Desire for a Budget Neutral Paid Family Leave Plan

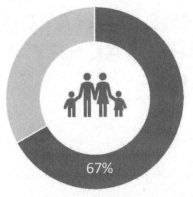

67% of Americans believe a paid family leave plan should remain budget neutral.

Source: Independent Women's Forum Poll, May 7, 2019.
Figure based on a national representative poll conducted by Heart and Mind Strategies for Independent Women's Forum of 2,010 Americans measuring attitudes toward federal paid leave policy and various proposals to expand access to paid time off from work.

on their Child Tax Credit (CDCD). The bill would allow parents to use the credit to help cover the costs of having or adopting a child.

Senator Cassidy, as he continues to work on getting the paid family leave bill passed, said that President Trump won the 2016 presidential election because more people believed that he cared about the average working American's plight more than did former secretary of state Hillary Clinton. Cassidy cited the president's forceful action on issues like the opioid crisis. "President Trump won because people were more convinced that he cared more about kitchen table issues than Hillary Clinton. That is clear," he told Breitbart News. Cassidy noted that President Trump has been the "ultimate force" behind kitchen table issues for Republicans.

37.

TRUMP HAS DONATED HIS ENTIRE SALARY AS PRESIDENT

As of March 3, 2020, the coronavirus had claimed the lives of nine Americans, with every one of those deaths occurring in Washington State. While the rest of the country was slowly coming to grips with the fact that we were in the throes of a global pandemic, President Trump had donated his fourth-quarter 2019 salary to the Department of Health and Human Services (HHS). The $100,000 in salary would go to HHS "to support the efforts being undertaken to confront, contain, and combat coronavirus," said White House press secretary Stephanie Grisham.

Donating his presidential salary fulfills one of the many promises Donald Trump made during his campaign for president. "The first thing I'm going to do is tell you that if I'm elected president, I'm accepting no salary, OK?" Trump said in November 2015 during a campaign event in Rochester, New Hampshire. "That's no big deal for me." Trump had built his ten-figure fortune as a developer and real estate mogul with a multinational portfolio of properties, hotels, and golf clubs, and as a reality television star. He ranked, at the time, at number 405 on *Forbes* magazine's list of the world's billionaires, with an estimated fortune of $4.1 billion.

The president has donated his salary to an array of federal agencies, the motivation for many of them being a mix of his personal and political proclivities. For instance, Trump's third-quarter 2018 donation to the National Institute on Alcohol Abuse and Alcoholism, a federal agency that researches alcoholism, was clearly motivated by the death of his older brother Fred Trump Jr., who had long suffered from alcoholism and died in 1981 at age forty-three from alcohol-related issues. Trump has never been shy about broaching his lifelong abnegation of alcohol. "I can honestly say I've never had a beer in my life," he joked to reporters in October 2018, while defending then–Supreme Court nominee Brett Kavanaugh. "Can you imagine, if I had, what a mess I'd be? I'd be the world's worst."

The president has made building a wall along the interior of the U.S.-Mexico border a centerpiece of his campaign. So, it only made sense that he dedicated a portion of his salary in 2018 to the Department of Homeland Security to help build that wall.

President Trump's Salary Donations

2017

Ql: National Park Service (for maintenance of a Civil War site)

Q2: Department of Education (for a science, technology, engineering, and math camp for children)

Q3: Department of Health and Human Services (for a public awareness campaign about opioid addiction)

Q4: Department of Transportation (for an infrastructure grant program)

2018

Q1: Veterans Administration (for a number of caregiver programs)
Q2: Small Business Administration (for Emerging Leaders, a seven-month intensive program for veterans)
Q3: National Institutes of Health
Q4: Department of Homeland Security

2019

Q1: U.S. Department of Agriculture (for outreach programs)
Q2: HHS/Office of the Surgeon General (for a health advisory)
Q3: Office of the Assistant Secretary of Health (for the opioid crisis)
Q4: Department of Health and Human Services (for "efforts being undertaken to confront, contain, and combat coronavirus," according to White House press secretary Stephanie Grisham)

2020

QI: Department of Health and Human Services (for the development of "new therapies for treating and preventing COVID-19 so we can safely re-open," according to White House press secretary Kayleigh McEnany)

The White House announced in November 2019 that the president was donating his third-quarter salary "to continue the ongoing fight against the opioid crisis." Taking on the scourge of opioid addiction is yet another pillar of the Trump administration.

Presidents are required by the Constitution to take a salary. Trump is the fourth president to donate his salary. George Washington, wealthy in his own right, donated most of his $25,000 salary. Herbert Hoover was already a millionaire when he was sworn into office as the thirty-first president on March 4, 1929. Hoover donated much of his $100,000 salary to various charities and even gave some to members of his staff. John F. Kennedy, who inherited millions, also donated his presidential salary to charity. "It cost me billions of dollars to be president, and I am so happy I did it because who cares?" Trump said in March 2020 during a coronavirus task force daily briefing. "I am really happy with the job that we're doing, and I'm really glad that this team and me are here."

38.

TRUMP HALTED THE FUNDING OF INTERNATIONAL ORGANIZATIONS THAT FUND OR PERFORM ABORTIONS

When Donald Trump announced his candidacy for president of the United States in the summer of 2015, many Americans—especially skeptical Republicans and conservatives—thought that the New York real estate billionaire might espouse liberal beliefs on social issues from abortion to religious freedom. However, pro-life leaders have lauded Trump for leading one of the most pro-life administrations in decades—if not ever. In the early days of his tenure, President Trump announced that he would sign an executive order that would mandate that aid to non-governmental organizations (NGOs) be prohibited from funding abortions. The order expands the policy to nearly all global health assistance funding.

Breitbart News reported that, within days of his inauguration, the president signed the executive order that had reinstated the Mexico City Policy, which bans American taxpayer dollars for the provision or promotion of abortions around the world. President Ronald Reagan established the Mexico City Policy in 1984 at the United Nations population conference, held in Mexico City. Every

Republican since Reagan has reinstituted the policy; however, every Democratic president has rescinded it. The reinstatement of the Mexico City Policy meant that billions in foreign aid appropriated to the U.S. Agency for International Development (USAID), the Department of Defense (DOD), and other organizations must be allocated according to Trump's executive order. David Brody of CBN News noted that prior versions of the Mexico City Policy applied only to family-planning assistance provided by the DOD and USAID. "That was roughly $600 million," Brody wrote. He added that the expanded Mexico City Policy now applies to a wider pool of foreign aid worth $8.8 billion.

One White House official noted that the president's Mexico City Policy ensures that NGOs that don't accept the United States' pro-life policy will not receive its taxpayers' money in the form of foreign aid. Pro-life leaders praised the Trump executive order. Marjorie Dannenfelser, president of the pro-life Susan B. Anthony List, said that the action is one of the many reasons that the pro-life community moved to get Trump elected. Dannenfelser said that the executive action will ensure that the American government will not promote NGOs that enthusiastically promote as well as perform abortions. Lila Rose, the president of Live Action, thanked President Trump for ending "taxpayer subsidies" to NGOs that perform abortions.

Not content with the Trump executive order, Secretary of State Mike Pompeo announced in March 2019 that the Trump administration would expand and more fully implement its commitment to ensure that American taxpayers are not forced to fund or promote abortions across the globe. "We can achieve . . . all the global health objectives that are so important, so imperative, the great work that many of these foreign NGOs do, without running the risk that they'll be used to perform abortions or advocate for abortions," Pompeo said. The Trump administration's expanded policy ensures that NGOs will have to prove to the State Department that they are not performing or advocating for others to obtain abortions. This expanded policy would eliminate virtually all the loopholes in the Mexico City Policy.

Family Research Council president Tony Perkins said in March 2019 that the abortion industry has always pursued taxpayer dollars. Jeanne Mancini, president of March for Life, said in March 2019, "Taxpayer dollars should not fund abortion here or abroad, and respecting the inherent dignity of the unborn person goes hand in glove with our country's foreign assistance and humanitarian work. The Secretary's courageous leadership on the implementation of this policy will assure its proper oversight and help advance the protection and empowerment of human persons at all stages in our international global health assistance initiatives."

A January 2019 Marist poll found that 75 percent of Americans oppose taxpayer funding of abortion abroad, with only 21 percent in favor. The data showed that 94 percent of Republicans, a whopping 80 percent of Independents, and even 56 percent of Democrats oppose taxpayer funding of abortions overseas. Dannenfelser said in March 2019 that the Trump administration has shown "strong leadership in stopping the exportation of abortion around the world on American taxpayers' dime.

"The American people have clearly and consistently voiced their opposition to taxpayer funding of the abortion industry, both at home and abroad," Dannenfelser added.

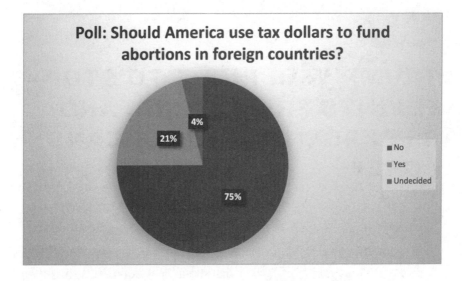

President Trump has continued to make history as one of the most pro-life presidents ever. He became the first president to speak at the March for Life in January 2020 on the National Mall.

> All of us here today understand an eternal truth. Every child is a precious and sacred gift from God. Every life brings love into this world, every child brings joy to a family. Every person is worth protecting, and above all, we know that every human soul is divine, and every human life born and unborn is made in the holy image of almighty God.
> —Donald Trump at the March for Life, January 2020

39.

TRUMP WAS RIGHT TO STOP FLIGHTS FROM CHINA, AND 95 PERCENT OF AMERICANS AGREE

When it comes to President Trump, there seem to be few things that Americans can agree on. He is either an earnest populist fighting for the little guy or a power-hungry con artist, a fearless truth-teller with little regard for niceties or an incorrigible boor. This divide, fueled in part by Trump's insistence on being constantly available to the American public through his Twitter account, has led to bitterly partisan, and sometimes mediocre, approval ratings. No American thinks Trump is "just okay."

So, it may have come as something of a surprise in March 2020, when Trump was more present than ever, speaking on television nightly in response to a global catastrophe, that he reached his highest-ever approval ratings. During the week of March 26, the RealClearPolitics poll average—which takes major national polls and aggregates them to come up with, as the name implies, an average presumably closer to reality than any of the individual polls—documented Trump's approval rating at 47 percent. His disapproval rating at the time was at 49.5 percent, second only to Trump's disapproval the month after his inauguration.

Fueling this, said a Pew Research Center survey published that same week, was support for the president's response to the Chinese coronavirus epidemic. On January 20, China revealed the domestic issue that had been secretly circulating in the country for months. Trump initially ordered ports of entry to reject individuals who had been in China in the past fourteen days; he added Europe to the ban in March after stratospheric growth in the number of coronavirus cases there.

A whopping 95 percent of Pew respondents said in a poll that they agreed that "restricting international travel to the U.S." was necessary to contain the spread of the virus. Even 94 percent of self-identified Democrats agreed with the measure. The poll also found Trump's job approval increasing by ten percent among black and Hispanic respondents, who often lean Democratic and consistently express more skepticism toward Trump than white voters.

The increase in support, for both the president and a key policy decision he made, during a time of crisis could suggest that the American public was being exposed to a significantly different media diet than the one they had available before the pandemic—one more favorable to the president, as often occurs with media coverage during crises. Even President George W. Bush, whom the left regularly compared to Adolf Hitler, received lukewarm and even positive coverage during the early days after the September 11, 2001, terrorist attacks.

Trump has not been quite as lucky. On the contrary, the president's every policy decision regarding the virus has faced an unrelenting barrage of insults and hysteria from both a press corps tasked with keeping Americans informed, and many of the powers that be in American politics. And no decision received more such scrutiny than his proclamation on January 31 to ban travelers who had visited China in the past fourteen days from entering the United States—a day after the World Health Organization (WHO) declared the outbreak a Public Health Emergency of International Concern (PHEIC).

The WHO has since upgraded the viral outbreak from a PHEIC to a pandemic—an epidemic affecting the entire world at the same time. It waited for China to claim that its own epidemic had ended *before* making the status modification. Prior to doing so, China announced that "mild" coronavirus cases did not count toward its official tally. Beijing never defined what distinguished a "mild" case from a severe one. Scientists believe the first case of COVID-19—a deadly pathogen that causes shortness of breath, fever, cough, and, eventually, pneumonia—was diagnosed in Wuhan, in central China, in November 2019. The Chinese Communist Party failed to make the discovery public until January 20, 2020, and shut down Wuhan only after 5 million people had left to travel for the Lunar New Year holiday.

Despite the undisputed origin of the virus, Democrats and left-wing media declared Trump's decision to limit travel from China "racist" and "xenophobic." This despite the fact that it targeted no particular race or ethnic identity and that it banned individuals from any country if they had been in China, not just direct-from-China travelers. Many couched their criticism of Trump in the fact that the WHO repeatedly demanded the world not close its ports of entry to Chinese travelers. "Countries must inform WHO about travel measures taken, as required by the IHR (International Health Regulations). Countries are cautioned against actions that promote stigma or discrimination, in line with the principles of Article 3 of the IHR," the organization asserted on January 30.

Director-General Dr. Tedros Adhanom Ghebreyesus again demanded that countries keep their doors open to Chinese travelers a week later. "We reiterate our call to all countries not to impose restrictions that unnecessarily interfere with international travel and trade," Tedros asserted. "Such restrictions can have the effect of increasing fear and stigma, with little public health benefit." Tedros, who is not a medical doctor, rose to the leadership of the WHO thanks to the effusive backing of the Chinese government. Multiple U.S. senators have called into question his relationship with Beijing, given the influx of $13.6 billion into the Ethiopian government from the Chinese Communist Party while he was prime minister.

With the green light from Tedros, the American left went to work attacking Trump. "This is a virus that happened to pop up in China. But the virus doesn't discriminate between Asian versus non-Asian," Representative Ami Bera (D-CA) told *Politico*, railing against the travel ban. "In our response we can't create prejudices and harbor anxieties toward one population." The *New York Times*, in an opinion piece by travel writer Rosie Spinks, implied that saying the coronavirus itself was dangerous to the health of human beings was racist. "The coronavirus travel ban is unjust and doesn't work anyway," Spinks, who did not in her short bio on the *New York Times* page indicate any background in epidemiology, confidently declared.

"Coronavirus shares something in common with other kinds of civil disruption, natural disasters or emergencies that affect localized travel industries: Its destructive power lies not in the actual risk but in the perception of that risk," Spinks argued. "Numerous experts have said that the majority of people who contract coronavirus will experience it as a respiratory infection they will fully recover from. But the extreme reactions—the canceling of flights, closing of borders and level-four travel warnings—seem more appropriate for something much worse." Spinks contended that the true threat was in America's "political moment dominated by xenophobic rhetoric and the building of walls."

Then there was Joe Robinette Biden Jr. Few used more deranged rhetoric to brand Trump's travel limits as racist than the presumptive Democratic presidential nominee. "This is no time for Donald Trump's record of hysteria and xenophobia—hysterical xenophobia—and fearmongering to lead the way instead of science," Biden proclaimed in Iowa on February 1. He made a similar statement on Twitter: "We are in the midst of a crisis with the coronavirus. We need to lead the way with science—not Donald Trump's record of hysteria, xenophobia, and fear-mongering.

"He is the worst possible person to lead our country through a global health emergency," said Biden, who has repeatedly referred to the coronavirus as the "Luhan virus," apparently confusing the Chinese city of Wuhan with a Korean pop star.

The backlash to Trump also took the form of protesting his referring to the virus as "Chinese," which Trump justified by noting that the virus had originated in China. A little over a month after Trump instated the travel ban, there were arguments that it did not work. Citing WHO epidemiologist Bruce Aylward, the leftist outlet *Vox* claimed, "Travel bans aren't going to stop community spread in the U.S." Perhaps the most prominent doctor responding to the coronavirus crisis at the national level, Dr. Anthony Fauci, director of the National Institute of Allergy and Infectious Diseases, has repeatedly dismissed this assertion, crediting the travel bans for keeping Americans safe. His responses on several news programs compared the United States to Italy, so his responses often framed the situation in comparison to that country, the worst affected in Europe.

By March 2020, the world had been aware of the coronavirus for about two months, and projections seeking to estimate infection rates and death tolls in America were grim. China was lying about its numbers, claiming the worst was over in Wuhan, while countries like Italy and Spain mourned the dead as their government-run healthcare systems chose who deserved to live or die. Panicked observers assumed that it was only a matter of time before similar scenes of overwhelmed hospital officials telling the elderly to go die at home played out across the Atlantic. "The president's decision to essentially have a major blocking of travel from China, that already had an effect of not seeding the way, in Europe—Italy didn't do that. And my—I feel so badly because I have so many friends there. They're getting hit hard," Fauci told *Meet the Press* in March. "What we're doing now with the other travel restrictions—so you block infections from coming in. And then within is when you have containment and mitigation. And that's the reason why the kinds of things we're doing that may seem like an overreaction will keep us away from that worst-case scenario."

"One of the things we did right was, very early, cut off travel from China to the United States. Outside of China where it origi-nated, the countries in the world that have it are through travel," Fauci said a week later on MSNBC. "Our shutting off travel from China, and more recently travel from Europe, has gone a long way to not seeding very, very intensively the virus in our country. Unfor-tunately, Italy did not do that. They had an open border."

"If you look at the dynamics of the outbreak in Italy, we don't know why they are suffering so terribly," Fauci said that same week-end, this time on CBS's *Face the Nation*. "But there's a possibility, and many of us believe, that early on they did not shut out as well the input of infections that originated in China and came to different parts of the world."

By mid-March 2020, 41,654 people had died globally of corona-virus complications. Given estimates that the real death toll in Iran is five times the government's claims and China's real death toll may be as much as twelve times the official figures, that global death toll of 41,654 might be a gross underestimation.

40.

TRUMP SHUT DOWN CHINA'S HOPES TO TAKE OVER AMERICA'S TELECOM INFRASTRUCTURE VIA HUAWEI

China has been ripping America off for decades. From currency manipulation to stealing intellectual property (IP) and undercutting manufacturing wages, China is willing to stop at nothing to destroy American business. Their labor practices fall just short of slavery; Chinese plants have installed suicide nets to catch workers who try to commit suicide by jumping out of windows. In many cases, our high-tech industry is more than happy to cooperate with the communist country. Apple's partners produce iPhones in the factories that use suicide nets. Google was designing a censored search engine called "Project Dragonfly" that would have helped the Chinese government root out dissidents. A slew of Silicon Valley outfits do business with the communists, sell their products to the government, or import Chinese workers on work visas instead of paying Americans standard wages.

Of course, there are anomalies. In December 2019, Apple expressed "deep concerns" that Chinese employees it accused of stealing trade secrets would flee to China. But for the most part, Silicon

Valley is happy to make deals with the communist devil because it's good for the bottom line to be in China's pocket. All this economic activity with Silicon Valley set the stage for one of President Donald Trump's most dramatic showdowns with the political power brokers in Beijing: Trump's decisive action against Huawei. The first question many people have to this day is, "What the heck is Huawei?"

It's okay if you aren't familiar with Huawei (pronounced wah-whey). One reason Huawei isn't a household name in the U.S. is that it has never had much of a presence as a consumer brand in America. As of 2018, Huawei held the second-biggest share of the smartphone market outside the United States; they were right behind Samsung. There are quite a few countries where the iPhone isn't as popular as it is in the United States, making Huawei a huge player in the Android market.

Huawei's other business is in heavy-duty networking and telecom equipment, the type of equipment that allows Zoomers (Generation Z-ers) to upload videos of silly dances to TikTok while they simultaneously watch Netflix and download books like this one on Kindle. In other words, Huawei is one of just several companies poised to control the beating heart of America's digital economy. Other big players in the space include European companies Ericsson and Nokia. America sadly sold its industry out to the Chinese and others long ago.

There are a lot of problems with Huawei. For one, like so many Chinese companies, it has a reputation for stealing intellectual property and trade secrets from its competitors. A federal indictment unsealed in February 2020 accuses the company of a "decades-long" pattern of racketeering (more on that later).

> The indictment charged Huawei with implementing a bonus program to brazenly reward employees who stole valuable information from other companies. Quite a few of those bonuses must have paid out, because DOJ judged the alleged intellectual property theft campaign to have been "successful" enough to help Huawei "drastically cut its research costs and associated delays, giving the company a significant and unfair competitive advantage."
>
> —Breitbart's John Hayward

Huawei also participates in other shady business schemes considered standard practice in China. For example, it has undercut competitors using money obtained from China's state-controlled banks at artificially low rates.

The single biggest problem with Huawei is that it has direct ties to the communist government of China. As Acting Secretary of Defense Patrick Shanahan explained in the summer of 2019, "The integration of civilian businesses with the military is too close. China has national policies and laws where data is required to be shared. When I look at that situation, it's too much risk. . . . You can't trust those networks are going to be protected."

Shanahan was commenting on the potential of the Chinese government to completely infiltrate America's telecom system. This became an even bigger threat as next-generation 5G wireless technology appeared on the horizon. China was salivating at the chance to blanket the United States in Huawei 5G tech, which would allow them to listen in on your conversations at any time. The idea must have been more appealing to the communist country than a giant bowl of fresh bat soup.

The ability for China to spy using Huawei tech isn't speculation. Robert O'Brien, the national security adviser to President Donald Trump, explained to the *Wall Street Journal*, "We have evidence that Huawei has the capability secretly to access sensitive and personal information in systems it maintains and sells around the world." Another official told the *Journal*, "Huawei does not disclose this covert access to its local customers, or the host nation national security agencies."

For decades, America looked the other way as Huawei robbed our high-tech companies of their technology and used it to spy. The election of Donald Trump changed everything. He has taken on Huawei. One of Trump's gambits was targeting the company's CFO, Meng Wanzhou. Wanzhou was hit with serious charges of breaking U.S.-imposed sanctions against Iran by lying to banks about Huawei's relationship with the country. And charging Wanzhou criminally sends a searing message to the company because she's the CEO's daughter.

Huawei is also facing the aforementioned federal racketeering charges. Trump's message to China and Huawei here is simple: "If you act like gangsters, we'll charge you like gangsters." Federal officials are using RICO statutes on China, just like they did against La Cosa Nostra in decades past.

In May 2019, Trump issued an executive order protecting America's telecom infrastructure from foreign infiltration. It doesn't mention Huawei and China, but that's exactly who it was aimed at.

Here's how former White House press secretary Sarah Huckabee Sanders explained it in a statement:

> **The President has made it clear that this Administration will do what it takes to keep America safe and prosperous, and to protect America from foreign adversaries who are actively and increasingly creating and exploiting vulnerabilities in information and communications technology infrastructure and services in the United States. This Executive Order declares a national emergency with respect to the threats against information and communications technology and services in the United States and delegates authority to the Secretary of Commerce to prohibit transactions posing an unacceptable risk to the national security of the United States or the security and safety of United States persons.**

Trump has also hit our allies who foolishly plan to continue doing business with Huawei. Former ambassador to Germany Richard Grenell said in early 2020 that Trump instructed him "to make clear that any nation who chooses to use an untrustworthy 5G vendor will jeopardize our ability to share intelligence and information at the highest level."

In May 2019, Trump placed the company on the "entity list," which means that American companies need all sorts of federal approval to sell a single chip or software package to Huawei. China expert Gordon Chang explained this move on SiriusXM's *Breitbart News Tonight*:

The Trump administration, in the middle of May, added Huawei to the Commerce Department's entity list, and that means for technology covered by export control regulations, no American company can have a transaction with Huawei—cannot sell to Huawei or license to Huawei— unless they get a license from Commerce.

Essentially this is a death sentence because Huawei is dependent on a couple of things: it's dependent on U.S. chips, and it's also dependent on Google for its Android operating system for its cell phones.

Will this move mean the end of Huawei? Many China and tech experts are doubtful. The Chinese government will find a way to prop up Huawei. After all, it's a great intelligence gathering tool! Whether Huawei lives or dies, it's clear that Donald Trump is dedicated to keeping its snooping hardware out of America's 5G infrastructure. And that means your social media accounts and online communications, along with those of America's most senior officials, are a little less likely to end up on the desks of Chinese intelligence officers in Beijing.

41.

TRUMP RECEIVED THE BIPARTISAN JUSTICE AWARD HONORING HIS CRIMINAL JUSTICE REFORM EFFORTS

Republicans have traditionally been the party of law and order. Donald Trump isn't a traditional Republican. He employed some of his trademark political jujitsu by enacting the most substantial criminal justice reform bill in decades. In December 2018, Trump signed the First Step Act, a rare moment of bipartisan support for legislation that featured vehement Democratic opposition to Trump's agenda.

First Step Act Criminal Justice Reforms

- Limits the use of restraints on federal prisoners who are pregnant or in postpartum recovery
- Reduces mandatory minimum prison sentences for some nonviolent repeat drug offenders
- Permits reduced penalties for some nonviolent, cooperative drug offenders with limited criminal records
- Limits juvenile solitary confinement

The president's support and signing of the First Step Act led the 20/20 Bipartisan Justice Center to honor President Trump with the "Bipartisan Justice Award" in October 2019. The 20/20 Bipartisan Justice Center is a group founded by 20 black Republicans and 20 black Democrats in 2015. Every year, it recognizes a public servant who works with members across the political aisle to achieve criminal justice reform. The award was presented at the 2019 Second Step Presidential Justice Forum, which was held at Benedict College, one of the approximately 100 historically black colleges and universities (HBCUs) in the country.

This meant that almost every Democratic presidential candidate was scheduled to attend the criminal justice event to see Trump receive his criminal justice award—when they were passed over for it. The Democratic candidates present were: Former representative John Delaney (D-MD), Senator Cory Booker (D-NJ), South Bend, Indiana, mayor Pete Buttigieg, Senator Kamala Harris (D-CA), Senator Amy Klobuchar (D-MN), former vice president Joe Biden, Senator Elizabeth Warren (D-MA), former Housing and Urban Development (HUD) secretary Julián Castro, Representative Tulsi Gabbard (D-HI), and Senator Bernie Sanders (I-VT).

During his speech at the 20/20 Bipartisan Justice Center, President Trump said that the First Step Act serves as a victory for people of all backgrounds and political beliefs. "My goal has been to give a voice to the voiceless and to make Washington see and hear those who have been made to feel silent and to feel invisible," the president said. "Although criminal justice reform was not a theme of my campaign initially, when I came into office, I heard from countless leaders and listened to many diverse points of view, including to our great church leaders and religious leaders. Everyone from governors to law enforcement officers, faith-based ministries. They all came to see me—asked me to fight on behalf of this forgotten community.

"I knew criminal justice reform was not about politics. I'm, to this day, not sure that what I did was a popular thing or an unpopular thing, but I know it was the right thing to do."

Trump continued, telling the story of Alice Johnson, a woman who was reformed by the federal justice system:

Alice had already served twenty-two years for a first-time, nonviolent drug offense. And she was going to be in prison for, it looked like, at least another twenty-eight years. That's her whole life. During her time in prison, Alice became a minister and mentored fellow inmates. She's an incredible woman. She took responsibility for her actions, but her sentence was simply not proportionate to her crime. And that's why I commuted Alice's sentence.

And I'll never forget the scene: She came out of prison, and there were her children, all grown up: big, strong guys; beautiful, really beautiful, incredible women with such love in their hearts. And they embraced and they kissed and they hugged and they cried outside of this big, monstrous prison . . .

I knew in that moment that I made the right decision. And we're all delighted that Alice is with us. She's been such an incredible representative. In fact, sometime I'm going to sit her down and ask what is it that you do? Please explain it to me, Alice, because I'd like to have a little bit

of what you have. [Laughter.] But she has been—she's got an incredible warmth and passion. And she really is a very special person. I've gotten to know her.

"I never in my wildest dreams would have thought that I'd be standing before such a group as this. What an honor," Johnson said. "I represent, as you see my face here, see the faces of the ones that you will never see unless we come together; unless we come together to act to cause other families to be reunited the way that I was reunited with my family," she added. "It was only by the grace of God that our president's heart was touched by my story and signed papers to commute my sentence."

President Trump said during his speech that criminal justice serves as a greater part of his America First policy vision, in which men and women, Americans of every race and creed, could benefit from combating illegal immigration, ending America's "forever wars," and fighting trade policies that outsource American jobs.

Trump explained:

For decades, politicians of both parties put their own interests ahead of your interests and put the interests of foreign nations ahead of the interest of our nation.

Our leaders spent $8 trillion on wars in the Middle East, but they allowed our great cities to fall into tragic decay and disrepair. For the cost of one year of war in the Middle East, we could have given scholarships to every child at every inner-city school in America and had tremendous numbers of dollars left over. Politicians drained America's wealth policing ancient tribal conflicts overseas, while

leaving generations of African American children trapped in failing government schools and in failing inner cities.

The same Washington establishment enacted ruinous trade policies that shuttered our factories and shipped our jobs very far away to other countries. More than half a million African Americans lost good-paying manufacturing jobs after the twin disasters of **NAFTA** and China's entrance into the World Trade Organization. That was a bad day.

At the same time, lawmakers and corporations joined forces to push immigration policies that hurt working-class Americans of all backgrounds. Many politicians fight harder in Congress for illegal immigrants than they do for United States citizens.

My administration will always put American communities first. On issue after issue, politicians raked in cash from special interests while selling out our nation's workers and our nation's great families.

Trump concluded, "Under this administration, the great betrayal of the American worker is over. After years of rebuilding—[applause]—thank you. After years of rebuilding foreign countries, we are finally rebuilding our country, renewing our cities, and securing our neighborhoods, and protecting our own forgotten communities."

42.

TRUMP DEFENDED THE FREE SPEECH RIGHTS OF CAMPUS CONSERVATIVES

As soon as Donald Trump famously came down that escalator and declared his candidacy for president in the summer of 2015, his supporters were targeted for political violence. There have been hundreds of documented acts of political violence or threats of violence against President Trump, his supporters, and conservative Americans—as when, to add insult to injury, Jussie Smollett framed Trump supporters with his hate crime hoax. Remember how downtown Chicago was suddenly MAGA country until it wasn't?

Violence Against Trump Supporters

- **July 2016: The Jacksonville Sheriff's Office said surveillance video caught the beating of a sixty-eight-year-old Vietnam veteran at a local gas station after saying he was going to vote for Donald Trump.**

- **January 2017: A Trump supporter was beaten unconscious at the Portland International Airport.**
- **June 2017: A Bernie Sanders campaign volunteer opened fire on dozens of Republican members of Congress, in Alexandria, Virginia, wounding Representative Steve Scalise (R-AL), two police officers, a congressional staffer, and a lobbyist.**
- **November 2017: Senator Rand Paul is beaten by his neighbor and suffers six broken ribs.**
- **March 2018: A female Trump supporter is attacked while protesting the Oscars in Los Angeles.**
- **October 2019: Video footage shows protesters punching Trump supporters outside the president's rally in Minneapolis.**
- **February 2020: A teenage supporter of President Trump is slapped at a polling station in New Hampshire.**

But there is another type of harassment of Trump supporters and conservatives in general that has rapidly picked up steam since Trump came to power but has been all but ignored by the mainstream press. I'm talking about the harassment of conservatives on campus. It's no secret that universities and college campuses have been islands of left-wing lunacy for decades. But it's only recently that they've become truly unhinged indoctrination mills, and if there's one thing no indoctrination center can stand, it's dissenting voices.

It's hard to briefly summarize the extent of the problems conservatives face on campus. The first logical place to look is the classroom. Technically, we go to college to attend classes, although I certainly missed a few in my day. So, what do conservatives face? According to the campus polling organization College Pulse, 73 percent of students with "strong Republican" political beliefs self-censor in the classroom to protect their grades. If they speak out in support of Trump—or generally disagree with the idea that America is a racist, sexist hellhole—they face retribution in the form of lower grades. I'm not exaggerating this point, that paints a picture tantamount to life in a communist country. Consider the survey response of a student at Kansas State, who wrote, "Professor the day after the presidential election kicked two students wearing MAGA hats out of class. I was appalled. We are all people, if someone disagrees with you, love them anyways."

The Atlantic, a most unlikely outlet to agree with me on practically *anything*, has also reported on self-censorship on campus. The left-wing outlet highlighted research from the University of North Carolina that backed up the College Pulse data showing conservatives make the awful decision to self-censor to avoid flunking. The UNC survey also showed that about 25 percent of leftist students believe it is perfectly fine to silence or suppress widely held views that they deem wrong. These are the people shutting down conservative speakers on campus.

Pause for a second and note the schools mentioned in this chapter. This isn't happening at Ivy League institutions or long-understood hotbeds of leftist insanity like Oberlin College. This is happening in Kansas and North Carolina!

Breitbart News documented 117 acts of campus violence and harassment against conservative students in November 2019. That sad statistic is expected to accelerate in the fall semester of 2020, in the run-up to the election. So many of the examples are outright violence, like when Turning Point USA (TPUSA) activist Hayden Williams was punched repeatedly in the face on the campus of UC Berkeley in 2019. But other examples involve threats designed to intimidate and silence conservatives. For example, a group of leftists at UT Austin threatened to dox any student joining the Young Conservatives of Texas or Turning Point USA clubs on campus. Wouldn't that make you think twice about joining a club, knowing your professors agree with the Gestapo-like thugs threatening you?

A third type of mistreatment campus conservatives face is outright harassment at the hands of university administrators. This may take the form of charging insanely high security fees for conservative student groups hoping to bring speakers like Ann Coulter to campus. A routine tactic for UC Berkeley and other University of California campus administrators is to simply not allow conservative groups to form in the first place. Drake University, a school in Des Moines, Iowa, denied the school's Turning Point USA chapter official recognition in November 2019. The decision was made in a private meeting without public comment. Drake's decision is especially shameful considering that the school had approved the Drake Comrades, a "communist and anarchist group," for the exact recognition it denied TPUSA.

All these categories of persecution and academic insanity are serious. For years, conservative campus groups, including Young

America's Foundation, outlets like Breitbart News, and a few groups like the Foundation for Individual Rights in Education (FIRE) have been vigilantly fighting for students' free speech rights. And they found a new and very powerful ally in President Donald Trump. He has embraced the youth wave washing over conservative politics and became aware that his young and very enthusiastic supporters were being maligned and victimized by the very institutions they (and their parents) pay tens of thousands of dollars to for a supposed education.

Trump took action in March 2019 with an executive order designed to defend free speech on campus. "Today, we are delivering a clear message to the professors and power structures trying to suppress, to keep young Americans and all Americans from challenging rigid far-left ideology," Trump said at the time. "People who are confident in their beliefs cannot censor others."

The executive order probably wouldn't deserve a chapter if it was just words from the president about how universities shouldn't behave like barbarians, but in typical Trump fashion, the order not only has teeth but delivers exactly the kind of pressure that publicly funded universities fear. You see, most universities and colleges collect large amounts of money in the form of tuition, but many of them rely on large sums of government money as well, often in the form of federal research grants. Those research grants total more than $35 billion a year. So, when Trump wanted colleges and universities to listen, he threatened their pocketbooks. "Taxpayer dollars should not subsidize anti–First Amendment institutions, and that's exactly what they are. Universities that want taxpayer dollars should promote free speech, not silence free speech," the president said.

Flanked by three college students, Trump signed the executive order with a clear message to higher education: "If a college or a university does not allow you to speak, we will not give them money; it's very simple."

The three students around Trump each have their own horror stories worth mentioning. Their accounts show that it isn't one group or action that universities are attacking, but rather a broad spectrum of beliefs, including those held by Christians and conservatives.

One of the students with Trump, Ellen Whitman, was a student at Miami University of Ohio, where she is the president for the school's chapter of the pro-life club Students for Life. Whitman and her club put up a "cemetery for the innocents" for several years, only to have it dismantled one year. The school called the display "dangerous and harmful" to other students. The second student with Trump at the signing was Katie Mullen, president of the TPUSA chapter at the University of Nebraska–Lincoln. Employees of the university harassed and even called the campus police on the club as it recruited new members on campus, a standard activity for every club at every university. The third student, Polly Olsen, successfully sued Northeast Wisconsin Technical College after the school stopped her from handing out Valentine's Day cards with religious messages like "Jesus loves you." The only thing that ruffles leftists' feathers as much as the "Orange Man" is Jesus!

Donald Trump takes the issue of free speech on campus seriously, and lawmakers have noticed. A throng of states are passing legislation requiring public universities that accept funds from the state government to ensure free speech on campus. Tennessee has taken the lead here but many states are following suit. Other efforts are happening at the federal level, with Senator Marsha Blackburn (R-TN) emerging as a champion for young conservatives.

43.

TRUMP BROKE UP OBAMA'S TITLE IX KANGAROO COURTS

What are the worst two words you could hear while in college? If you graduated toward the end of the first decade of the twenty-first century, you'd probably answer "pop quiz." That phrase likely scared the hell out of the average college student sitting in class before, say, 2011. That's the year our unelected overlords unleashed a new two-word terror: "Dear Colleague."

The Office for Civil Rights (OCR) within Obama's Education Department sent its infamous "Dear Colleague" letter to colleges and universities across the country on April 4, 2011. This three-page letter changed the lives of many male students and struck fear into the hearts of many more. The Dear Colleague letter instructed the roughly 7,000 colleges and universities in this country that receive some form of federal money to drastically change how they adjudicate accusations of sexual misconduct by students. I suggest you read the letter. It's available online. And it stands as a monument to the Obama administration's ability to contort practically anything into a nightmarish mess of bureaucratic as-ininities.

The letter dictated new terms for how schools would handle accusations of student-on-student sexual misconduct. The only way to properly describe the procedures in place at just about every college you can think of is "kangaroo court." On behalf of the many men whose educational dreams were crushed by this process, I sincerely wish this were a joke. Alas, the Obama-era edict created a cock-eyed reality on college campuses for the better part of a decade. Thanks to Obama & Co., universities were instructed to employ the lowest possible standard of proof in sexual assault cases, which in legal terms is referred to as the preponderance of evidence. In other words, school officials were being asked to meet a higher standard of proof to punish teenagers for cheating in class or getting a noise violation for a party than to brand them as sex criminals. Think that's crazy? It was merely the tip of the iceberg.

A second directive of the Dear Colleague letter insisted that ac-cusers could appeal a not guilty verdict ruled in favor of the person they accused of sexual misconduct. Who has ever heard of the plain-tiff getting to appeal a not-guilty verdict? In the American criminal justice system, that's called "double jeopardy" and it is unconstitu-tional. You'd think colleges and universities would be familiar with the Fifth Amendment of the Constitution. The letter also advised school administrators that these kangaroo court trials should be speedy. It actually suggested a sixty-day limit from charges made to verdict reached. Anything to make it harder for a broke college student to organize a proper response and defense to very serious charges, right? Sadly, inciting a speedy trial wasn't even the worst part. The OCR suggested that schools should not allow the cross-examination of the accuser. Every person charged with a crime in America has the right to cross-examine their accuser, except college students accused of not only rape, but practically any level of un-wanted sexual contact.

Under the campus kangaroo courts set up based on the

Obama-era rules, young men didn't have a prayer of a fair hearing. One high-profile example involved German exchange student Paul Nungesser, who was charged with rape as a student at Columbia University by fellow student Emma Sulkowicz. You may not recognize her name, but you may have heard of her being referred to as Mattress Girl. Sulkowicz carried around a mattress for the rest of her time at Columbia as an act of "performance art." She also became a national hero for feminists, fully backed and aided by Columbia, which actually gave her college credit for her numerous stunts. Meanwhile, Nungesser's college existence was consumed by Columbia's kangaroo court. He eventually sued the school and settled out of court.

> ## Reactions to Mattress Girl
>
> **Mattress Performance: Carry that Weight is almost certainly already one of the most important artworks of the year. I don't think that's a stretch to say.**
>
> **—Artnet**

> **One student at Columbia University in New York, a survivor of sexual assault, began carrying her mattress around campus. That image should haunt all of us.**
>
> **—Hillary Clinton**

> **The work Ms. Sulkowicz is making is strict and lean, yet inclusive and open ended, symbolically laden yet drastically physical.**
>
> *—New York Times*

Luckily for college students who already face a heap of hurdles on campus from skyrocketing tuition to leftist indoctrination, Donald Trump and his Education Secretary, Betsy DeVos, had a plan to rewrite the Obama-backed rules that make a mockery of the American justice system. DeVos introduced her new rules in November 2018, righting many of Obama's wrongs. DeVos didn't completely flip the rules on their head. There is still an emphasis placed on the seriousness of sexual misconduct on campus. DeVos said, "Throughout this process, my focus was, is, and always will be on ensuring that every student can learn in a safe and nurturing environment."

She instead created a balance, taking into account all students. Consider her words carefully here:

> **That starts with having clear policies and fair processes that every student can rely on. Every survivor of sexual violence must be taken seriously, and every student accused of sexual misconduct must know that guilt is not predetermined. We can, and must, condemn sexual violence and punish those who perpetrate it, while ensuring a fair grievance process. Those are not mutually**

exclusive ideas. They are the very essence of how Americans understand justice to function.

DeVos essentially returned commonsense standards of due process to their rightful place on U.S. campuses. Throughout the grievance process related to accusations of sexual misconduct, the accused student now has a presumption of innocence. Gee, what a concept! The accused is also guaranteed a written notice of the allegations against him, something that didn't always happen with the Obama-era rules. Crucially, the accused also have the right to review all evidence against them, and the right to cross-examine, subject to "rape shield" rules, just like in the real world. The style of cross-examination laid out by DeVos is very fair, especially considering the dicey situations young people can find themselves in. It doesn't involve students confronting each other but rather questions asked by their advisers, similar to a courtroom hearing in some respects.

The DeVos rules also set the definition of sexual harassment under Title IX as consistent with Supreme Court cases: "unwelcome conduct on the basis of sex that is so severe, pervasive, and objectively offensive that it effectively denies a person equal access to the school's education program or activity." Gone are the days of kangaroo court charges based on a student claiming another student looked at them for too long. DeVos summarized her reasoning for the changes thus, saying:

Far too many students have been forced to go to court to ensure their rights are protected because the Department has not set out legally binding rules that hold

schools accountable for responding to allegations of sexual harassment in a supportive, fair manner. By following proper legal procedures and receiving input on our proposed rule, we will ultimately have a final regulation that ensures that Title IX protects all students.

Betsy DeVos has demonstrated a desire to help all students and return colleges to a place of higher learning, not miniature Soviet blocs where easily offended hall monitors and busybodies are free to make campus life a living hell. In case you think DeVos considered her job just fixing up a system with a few minor flaws, I will leave you with one final quote from her: "Instead of working with schools, the prior administration weaponized the Office for Civil Rights." Has there ever been a better summary of the Obama administration?

44.

FROM HIS FIRST MONTH IN OFFICE, PRESIDENT TRUMP PRESIDED OVER THE LARGEST MANUFACTURING BOOM IN A FIRST TERM SINCE THE 1970S

President Donald Trump constantly committed to reviving American industry during his 2016 presidential campaign, promising that he'd bring back jobs that the country lost due to unfair trade deals. His loud appeals to blue-collar laborers went a long way toward putting him in the White House, even though they garnered ceaseless skepticism from the establishment media, mainstream economists, and his predecessor.

New York Times columnist Paul Krugman said weeks after Trump's election that the president would never bring back lost manufacturing jobs. Krugman declared that "nothing policy can do will bring back those lost jobs. The service sector is the future of work; but nobody wants to hear it." At a PBS town hall in June 2016, former president Barack Obama poured cold water on Trump's promise to restore a manufacturing sector that'd been slowly picked apart for decades. Obama contended that decades of America's diminished dominance in manufacturing was proof of a larger global trend. "Well, how exactly are you going to do that?" Obama asked rhetorically. "What exactly are you going to do? There's no answer to it. He just says, 'Well, I'm going to negotiate a better deal.' Well, what, how exactly are you going to negotiate that? What magic wand do you have? And usually the answer is, he doesn't have an answer." It was Barack Obama who oversaw a stagnant and declining manufacturing sector during his eight years in office. According to the U.S. Bureau of Labor Statistics (BLS), Obama's economy produced fewer than 100,000 manufacturing jobs across the nation during his last two years in office. In contrast to Obama, manufacturing jobs started soaring shortly after Trump assumed office in January 2017.

Forbes Reports More Manufacturing Jobs in the Trump Administration

Since the Trump Administration's red-tape-cutting policies and the tax cut and reform law passed in December 2017, manufacturers added 467,000 jobs, more than six times the 73,000 manufacturing jobs added in Obama's last two years.

Looking at Trump's first two years, the revised BLS data shows that more than two manufacturing jobs were added for every one job added in government at the federal, state, and local level. In contrast, under Obama, almost five government jobs were added for every one manufacturing job.

Since President Trump took office in January 2017, employment in manufacturing has increased 3.7 percent. During the last two years under President Obama, manufacturing payrolls grew by only 0.6 percent.

Justin Haskins, the editorial director and a research fellow at the Heartland Institute, noted in an op-ed in *The Hill* in January 2020 that Democratic lawmakers fundamentally misunderstand job creation. Instead, Haskins argues that what's necessary for the economy to flourish is to allow business owners to operate with minimal government interference.

"What Obama and others in the Democratic Party didn't understand—and judging by the rhetoric coming from the current batch of presidential candidates, still don't understand—is that you don't need a magic wand to grow the economy," Haskins wrote. "All that is required are policies that give individuals and businesses more power to operate freely and that limit efforts by inept, greedy government bureaucrats in Washington to meddle and manipulate markets they don't fully understand."

Haskins noted that the Trump administration had signed 16 bills to slash regulation and eliminated eight and a half rules for every new statute instituted. "Since January 2017, more than 480,000 manufacturing jobs have been added to the U.S. economy, following two decades of sharp losses," Haskins wrote. He explained that during President Clinton's final three years in office, the country lost more than 430,000 manufacturing jobs, and during George W. Bush's time in office, Americans lost millions of manufacturing jobs, even before the 2008 financial crisis. "Roughly 300,000 manufacturing jobs were lost during the eight years of the Obama administration, including minor losses in Obama's final year in office," Haskins emphasized. "In terms of the percentage of manufacturing job increases, the gains made thus far under the Trump administration surpass the performance in the first term of every president since the 1970s."

So much of Trump's manufacturing renaissance has occurred in the Rust Belt of Iowa, Minnesota, and Wisconsin—a critical swath of states that proved crucial to the working-class coalition President Trump relied on in November 2016. Pennsylvania has also experienced much of the manufacturing boom under Trump. Under Obama, the Keystone State, a big blue-collar bastion, lost more than 45,000 manufacturing jobs. During the early years of Trump's presidency, Pennsylvania gained roughly 23,000 manufacturing jobs.

Trump's appeal to blue-collar workers led to his 2016 win in Pennsylvania, which a Republican president had not won since George H. W. Bush's 1988 election nearly three decades earlier. Haskins described the manufacturing boom as "Trump's big reelection weapon."

"It turns out that you don't need incantations or even a 'magic wand' to improve manufacturing job growth. You do, however, need public policies in place that promote U.S. businesses, instead of punishing them with ever-higher taxes, regulations, and mandates,"

Haskins noted. "President Trump understands this reality, and he's poised to reap the benefits in 2020 as a result."

Trump and other Republicans have mocked Obama because Trump revived the economy that Obama could not, and went so far as to say could not be revived. Donald Trump Jr., the president's eldest son, said in September 2018, "Okay, remember when Obama said you need a magic wand to make that happen? Well, abracadabra, Obama. We're doing it."

"I guess I have a magic wand, 4.2 percent [GDP], and we will do MUCH better than this! We have just begun," President Trump fired back in September 2018.

45.

TRUMP'S FEDERAL AGENCIES ARE INVESTIGATING THE BIG TECH GIANTS' MONOPOLISTIC PRACTICES

There are some words in the English language that have practically no positive connotations. Take for example the word *probe*. I don't care if you are in the habit of turning lemons into lemonade, getting probed is *bad*. Probes are so bad that even the Silicon Valley Masters of the Universe shake in their boots when they receive letters from federal agencies. And that is exactly what is happening thanks to President Donald Trump.

Big Tech companies have largely been allowed to run wild since the day they were formed. Matters were made much worse during the Obama years, exacerbated by the cozy relationship between the administration and major Silicon Valley players like Facebook and Google. Google executives were not only some of the most frequent visitors to the Obama White House but the Internet conglomerate and the executive branch became something of a revolving door, trading employees throughout Obama's White House tenure. To put it simply, Silicon Valley has perfected a business model of ignoring inconvenient laws, referred to as "disruption" in the language of the Valley, and of ignoring customers, which they call "letting fires burn." The federal government appeared happy to look away as the tech industry—and Amazon specifically—on one hand laid waste to the retail sector, and on the other demolished Internet competition whenever smaller companies had the misfortune of getting in their way. Facebook and Google, I'm looking your way on this one.

Conservatives have been arguing for years about how best to beat back Big Tech's unimpeded monopolistic supremacy. Some on the right speak out in defense of the free market, only to change their tune when they get banned from a social media platform. Other conservatives, including those in Congress like Senators Marsha Blackburn (R-TN), Josh Hawley (R-MO), and Ted Cruz (R-TX), are taking a hard look at special protections the Masters of the Universe have long enjoyed under federal law—specifically, Section 230 of the Communications Decency Act. No matter where you stand on the issue of how to treat Big Tech, there is one thing that shouldn't be controversial: Big Tech companies should have to abide by the same laws of antitrust and anti-competitive behavior as every company in America. And, like every other company in America, they should be prohibited from defrauding their customers and suppliers.

Apparently, that's a revolutionary idea for the federal government. Donald Trump has brought a lot of revolutionary ideas to Washington, D.C., and enforcing laws on Silicon Valley appears to be one of them. Most of the action is happening at the Federal Trade Commission (FTC) and the Department of Justice (DOJ). Under President Trump, these agencies are giving Big Tech the scrutiny they've dodged for decades.

Take, for example, Amazon. Jeff Bezos started Amazon as a

bookseller in the mid-1990s. The company has since evolved into a behemoth selling, well, *everything*. And Amazon, following the aforementioned buzzword, *disruption*, hasn't kept too close an eye on what it's selling. For example, Apple alleged in a 2016 lawsuit that 90 percent of the Apple power accessories sold on Amazon were counterfeit. Makes you wonder what else you've bought off the site that's counterfeit. The FTC began investigating Amazon's anti-competitive practices in 2019. The agency questioned Amazon's competitors and suppliers over a variety of business practices. Some of the areas in question include its logistics and fulfillment services, which punished customers for selling products on other platforms by charging up to 75 percent more for logistics services on those orders. Second, Amazon aggressively markets its own branded products in competition with other popular products on the site. Finally, the FTC wanted to understand how Amazon's "Prime" bundles hurt competition by continually adding more services.

Instead of taking the Obama-era approach of putting Big Tech in charge of making sure Big Tech isn't breaking the rules, the FTC is listening to the small and medium-size businesses that are hurt by Amazon's dubious business practices. As reported by Bloomberg, Chris McCabe, a former Amazon executive who helps small businesses, said, "These conversations are going to keep happening. I've had several people ask me how to go to the FTC. I give them an email, and the FTC is taking their calls."

FTC Chairman Joe Simon is taking this seriously, unlike his predecessors. Speaking not only of Amazon but companies like Google and Facebook, Simon said the FTC would even consider busting up monopolies and duopolies if it becomes necessary. "It's not ideal because it's very messy. But if you have to you have to," Simon told Bloomberg. The DOJ, not wanting to miss the party, also started scrutinizing Big Tech in 2019. The agency's antitrust division said in a statement that it would be investigating "whether and how market-leading online platforms have achieved market power and are engaging in practices that have reduced competition, stifled innovation, or otherwise harmed consumers."

One of the agency's primary targets is Google. The Mountain View, California, company holds a virtual monopoly on web searches, controls the top two most-visited websites on the entire Internet (Google.com and YouTube.com), and dominates online marketing in a duopoly with Facebook that Amazon is just now edging into. One of the areas that the DOJ's probe of Google has focused on is that online ads duopoly. Google, for all intents and purposes, can decide what websites make ad revenue online. It is also one of the company's primary sources of revenue.

DOJ Probes Google's Advertising Business

Breitbart News tech reporter Lucas Nolan covered the DOJ's probe of Google and its advertising business in February 2020, writing:

The Justice Department has reportedly been posing detailed questions to Google's rivals as well as Google executives about how the firm's third-party advertising service works with publishers and advertisers. Google's advertising business was largely launched by the company's purchase of ad-tech firm DoubleClick in 2008. Many recent questions about the company's ad tech relate to moves Google has reportedly made to consolidate its power in the advertising industry.

The first move being investigated is Google's integration of its ad server, which is the leading tool for websites to place ad space for sale on their site. The second move was Google's decision to force advertisers to use its own tools to buy ad space on the video-sharing platform YouTube. Michael Nevins, chief marketing officer of Smart AdServer, which makes a rival ad technology to Google's, commented: "They are zooming in on the right topics, and that's a good thing."

As if the federal probe wasn't enough to make Google begin to understand it no longer calls the shots on behalf of all Americans, attorneys general of fifty states and territories are also investigating Google for anti-competitive practices that hurt businesses and individuals in their respective states. That's every state and territory in the Union except for California and Alabama. If you're reading this book in California or Alabama, this is a fantastic time to contact your state attorney general and ask them why they are willing to give Google a pass as they crush competition from smaller companies in your state. California is especially egregious as it is home to so many start-ups swept aside by Google, but we can safely assume the government of California lets Big Tech call the shots just like Obama did.

Of course, Facebook is under the federal microscope as well. Both the FTC and DOJ have expressed interest in Facebook, with the DOJ actively investigating Mark Zuckerberg's Internet giant since 2019. Facebook is under investigation for traditional monopolistic practices, like buying up competitors and crushing those that won't be bought by imitating their features. Zuckerberg proudly testified to Congress that the average smartphone user has eight different social media apps on their phone. But Facebook either owns or mirrors all eight. Between the Facebook app and its Facebook Messenger, WhatsApp, and Instagram apps, the social media giant pretty much covers the field. At the same time, Facebook has become the second-largest web advertising giant, sharing a duopoly with Google.

We don't yet know how these various investigations will play out but there is a tremendous positive here: The Masters of the Universe are being treated like the rest of industry. They are expected to follow federal law, instead of being allowed to make up regulations as they go and ignore laws that might stunt their growth. It took Donald Trump and law enforcement agencies under his direction to make some of the most powerful and wealthiest executives in America squirm.

46.

FOREIGN INVESTMENT IN THE USA HAS REACHED AN ALL-TIME HIGH UNDER DONALD TRUMP

Donald Trump's candidacy sent a resounding message to the rest of the world: America is back in business. The same Trump-promoted policies that unshackled American businesses, slashing red tape and tossing out pointless regulations, have made America a more attractive place for foreigners to invest their money. Numbers don't lie. President Trump successfully attracted investment in the United States through the first few years of his tenure. According to the National Taxpayers Union, foreign investment in the United States reached a record level of $35.5 trillion in 2018. As explained by the National Taxpayers Union, this includes $8.9 trillion of direct investment in factories and facilities, $8 trillion invested in the stock of American companies, and $6.3 trillion in Treasury securities.

Donald Trump advertised the United States as a refuge for profit to the global corporate community. He walked and talked of tough but fair deals. For example, the USMCA trade deal with Canada and Mexico will benefit all three nations.

There is a tendency among some center-right economists to downplay the importance of foreign investment in the United States.

#1

Home to the Largest Amount of Foreign Direct Investment (FDI) in the World

Source: UNCTAD (year end 2018)

U.S. JOBS
Supported by FDI:

200,000–600,000
100,000–200,000
75,000–100,000
25,000–75,000
5,000–25,000

"What does it help the average American if Japan buys treasuries or a French tycoon acquires $100 million in Apple shares?" they like to ask. Often left out is the third leg of foreign investment I mentioned earlier—investment in factories and facilities. That important part of the equation turns out to be a big benefit to the American worker.

One example of that benefit is Foxconn, the giant Taiwanese-based electronics company. They are one of Apple's primary partners to build iPhones, largely in China. Under Obama and his predecessors, it was treated as gospel that such companies would never operate in the United States. But Foxconn announced they are building a $10 billion plant in Wisconsin that will employ 13,000 Americans. They plan to make small liquid crystal display screens for devices like smartphones, tablets, and smart TVs.

Think about what that $10 billion investment by Foxconn will do for the residents of Wisconsin. It will improve the quality of life and lift up the entire economy of the region as businesses spring up to support the plant. In a perfect world, the fat paychecks these workers will be bringing home would have the name of an American company on them. But at the end of the day, the important part of a paycheck is the numbers going into Americans' bank accounts. Foxconn coming to the United States is another lever President Trump can apply to companies trying to outsource production to China and other countries. A theoretical phone call to an American CEO might go: "The Taiwanese are coming here, why are you taking your jobs to China?"

Foxconn isn't the only game in town either. Toyota and Mazda are building a joint plant in Alabama valued at $1.6 billion that will employ 4,000 workers. Car factories are great for the economy because wherever they open, an entire universe of car parts suppliers show up.

If foreign companies aren't building new factories, they are expanding existing facilities. In July 2018, BMW detailed plans to devote $600 million to scaling up its plant in South Carolina, adding 1,000 jobs. When you factor in all the American tradesmen building these factories, there are too many wins to count.

If a car dealership sells a BMW built in South Carolina by American workers, it contributes to the trade deficit with Germany, some economists still gripe. But that logic focuses purely on numbers on a spreadsheet measuring trade between the two countries. I'm much more interested in measuring the positivity for the American worker and local economies when a factory is built, providing high-paying jobs and new business opportunities for towns thought to have seen their best days pass.

47.

TRUMP'S AMERICA FIRST POLICIES HELPED LIFT CORPORATE PROFITS TO RECORD LEVELS

The economic miracle that has occurred during Donald Trump's first term in office produced corporate profits after taxes roughly equal to two historic highs during the Obama years. You must be thinking: *Corporations have frequently, for decades, worked against the America First wave Donald Trump rode into the White House.* That's true. Between the corporations rushing to do business with China, the Hollywood studios packing China-approved propaganda in our movies, marketers flooding TV with woke ads, and those companies in the pocket of the Democratic party, most Americans might not be particularly interested in cheering on their massive profits. But the difference between the record profits of the Obama years and the record profits under Trump is startling and worth closer examination.

According to the Federal Reserve Bank of St. Louis, corporate profits after tax for 2019 Q4 reached just over $1.9 trillion. That is basically equal to Obama's best quarter, 2014 Q3, which came in $10 billion higher, and just above 2012 Q1. When we're counting trillions, a few billion isn't much of a difference, so let's consider these three quarters equal. That's where the similarities end. Obama's record-profit quarters were part of the infamous jobless recovery, often called the "non-recovery recovery." As *Investor's Business Daily* pointed out in February 2013, right in the middle of Obama's record profits era, "when it comes to job creation, we are barely treading water."

If you look at Obama's economy throughout his presidency, "treading water" is an exceedingly kind judgment. Here are the facts about the economy Obama built during his eight years in office. Keep in mind that corporate profits were ballooning during that time, starting not long after the financial crisis of 2008.

The most important stat of Obama's presidency is not the unemployment rate, which fell (that's good) but the labor participation rate, which also fell (that's bad). Some 13.5 million people basically gave up on their chances of finding a job and settled into part-time work or long-term unemployment. The labor participation rate, a measure of how many people are working who could be working, fell from 65.8 percent to 62.8 percent during the Obama years. Basically, people weren't working no matter what the unemployment rate looked like.

Median household income was also stagnant under Obama. Certainly some fat cats and Silicon Valley mavens made out like bandits. But the average American was not tasting the success of those corporate profits.

The home ownership rate declined from 67.3 percent to 63.5 percent. Is there any more direct measurement of the American dream than owning a house? Perhaps the worst economic figure from the Obama era, especially for black and Latino Americans along with low-income whites, is the massive increase in food stamps. Some

32 million people received food stamps at the beginning of 2009, and that hit a peak of 47.8 million in December 2012. Right in the middle of soaring corporate profits, more Americans than ever were using food stamps to feed their families. To steal a common Trump exclamation, SAD!

After leading America to record corporate profits and record food stamp usage, Barack Obama doubted Donald Trump's ability to bring back jobs, like those in the manufacturing sector. Of course, Obama couldn't have been more wrong about Trump. That really became a trend for him, didn't it?

In reality, manufacturers added six times more jobs in Trump's first two years in office than were created in Obama's last two years. If that's not evidence of a "magic wand," I don't know what is.

Whole swaths of this book document the evidence that the levels of corporate profits achieved under Trump, often equal to those under Obama, came about the right way. In other words, there is strong evidence that these profits were good for America instead of China and a select cadre of corporate bigwigs.

Take, for example, the chapter on the wage growth of blue-collar workers under Trump, which reached record levels. They're a far cry from the Silicon Valley executives who profited under Obama. In fact, you'll find the business press complaining that profits are being hurt by wage growth and a competitive labor market. Those are good things for America, even if they are bad for a few CEOs. Median household income reached $63,179 in 2019, the highest level on record.

And let's not forget what happened to the money *after* the profits were earned. Under Obama, trillions piled up in tax havens like Ireland. After Trump's historic tax law overhaul, more than a trillion dollars of those corporate profits returned to the United States, providing a massive windfall for the American economy.

I said earlier that one of the most glaring signs of Obama's economic failures was the massive increase in food stamp usage. That was indicative of an economy failing to help the lower class raise themselves up, while also allowing the lower middle class to sink into despair.

Trump has turned that around too. The USDA reports that, as of the beginning of 2020, 6 million people are off food stamps during his presidency. There is a long way to go to get the people Obama abandoned back to work, but the right man is on the job.

48.

CYBERBULLYING PLUMMETED UNDER TRUMP AS MELANIA TRUMP'S ANTI-CYBERBULLYING INITIATIVE WENT FORWARD

The increased digitization of American culture coincided with a disturbing surge in reported cases of cyberbullying. A Comparitech survey released in March 2020 found that the percentage of parents reporting bullying had increased sharply in the United States from 15 percent in 2011 to 34 percent in 2016. But by 2018, the percentage had plummeted to 26 percent. The statistical free fall in reported cases of cyberbullying occurred over the course of a couple years that saw the American left, from the elite media to elected lawmakers, ceaselessly castigating President Trump as a bully (who had also likely committed treason in teaming up with the Kremlin to steal the 2016 election).

"How the Psychology of Cyberbullying Explains Trump's Tweets," read one *Politico* article, which treated its readers to an unbroken stream of unscientific silliness about how the president is (get this) "too old to be considered a cyberbully," and fits, instead, in the category of "'flamers,' 'trolls,' and 'cyber harassers.'"

Headlines About Donald Trump

- *Washington Post*: "How the Bully in Chief Is Turning America Nastier"
- *The New Yorker*: "How to Beat Trump, According to Experts on Middle-School Bullies"
- **CNN**: "The Roots of Trump's Bullying"
- *Politico*: "Trump the Bully"

Comparitech conducted 20,793 interviews between March and April 2018 across America and Canada before releasing their findings. The decline between 2016 and 2018 put America's cyberbullying at levels comparable to Belgium and Sweden. In 2016, during the Obama administration, America experienced the worst levels of cyberbullying, the group's data showed.

This data mirrors similar findings found in a 2018 Pew Research study that said a majority of teens, or 59 percent, experienced some form of cyberbullying. Pew found that:

- 42 percent experienced name-calling
- 32 percent were the subject of a false rumor
- 25 percent experienced explicit images they did not ask to receive
- 16 percent experienced physical threats
- 7 percent had graphic images shared without their consent

The Cyberbullying Research Center found that 28 percent of teens have been cyberbullied.

First Lady Melania Trump can take some credit for helping improve the state of cyberbullying in the United States. She made it clear before becoming first lady that tackling cyberbullying would be a focus for her office in the administration. Mrs. Trump began working to address the scourge of cyberbullying in the early days of her husband's presidency. "No child should ever feel hungry, stalked, frightened, terrorized, bullied, isolated, or afraid, with nowhere to turn," Mrs. Trump said in September 2017 in a speech in front of dozens of world leaders during the United Nations General Assembly. "We must teach each child the values of empathy and communication that are at the core of the kindness, mindfulness, integrity, and leadership, which can only be taught by example."

Mrs. Trump launched her antibullying campaign "Be Best" in May 2018. No surprise, the initiative was met with mockery by leftists online. Still, "Be Best" puts fighting cyberbullying at the center of the first lady's campaign, alongside combating opioid addiction and abuse.

"As a mother and as first lady, it concerns me that in today's fast-paced and ever-connected world, children can be less prepared to express or manage their emotions and oftentimes turn to forms of destructive or addictive behavior such as bullying, drug addiction or even suicide," the first lady said at a Rose Garden event.

"I feel strongly that as adults, we can and should be best at educating our children about the importance of a healthy and balanced life," Mrs. Trump said. "As we all know, social media can both positively and negatively affect our children. But too often, it is used in negative ways. When children learn positive online behaviors early on, social media can be used in productive ways and can affect positive change."

Like clockwork, left-wing outlets like CNN rushed to cast President Trump as a prime example of the kind of cyberbullying the first lady's program was meant to address. The *New York Times* even wrote a running list of the roughly 500 "people, places, and things" the president had allegedly insulted on Twitter. "Melania Trump Speaks at Anti-Cyberbullying Summit While Donald Trump Cyberbullies," one *Huffington Post* headline read. Mrs. Trump cut through the media's choreographed howl of fake rage and focused on improving the climate for America's children.

"I am well aware that people are skeptical of me discussing this topic," Melania Trump said in November 2018. "I have been criticized for my commitment to tackling this issue, and I know that will continue. But it will not stop me from doing what I know is right."

During a panel that featured youth activists, social media executives, and law enforcement, she said, "In today's global society, social media is an inevitable part of our children's daily lives. It can be used in many positive ways, but can also be destructive and harmful when used incorrectly."

"That is why Be Best chooses to focus on the importance of teaching our next generation how to conduct themselves safely and in a positive manner in an online setting," she added.

"By listening to children's ideas and concerns, I believe adults will be better able to help them navigate this often-difficult topic," she said. "Let's face it: Most children are more aware of the benefits and pitfalls of social media than some adults."

By 2019, anecdotal declines in bullying had begun to emerge. A survey of students in Utah's Tooele County School District schools found that bullying dropped in 2019 compared to the two previous years, according to the 2019 Student Health and Risk Prevention

(SHARP) on school climate and mental health. Furthermore, 80 percent of students said that they feel safe at school. Reported classroom disruptions went down by 7 percent in South Carolina's Florence County School District in August. Bullying and cyberbullying declined 31 percent. The local NBC affiliate reported that "attack [*sic*] on a student, whether verbal or physical, had the largest decrease from more than 1,400 student referrals to 700." Morgan County, Indiana, school districts reported low bullying numbers in October 2019. The *Los Angeles Times* reported in October 2019 that bullying of California Muslim students, who had been bullied because of their faith, saw "a sharp decline from the previous year."

49.

MEDIAN HOUSEHOLD INCOME REACHED $65,666 IN 2019, THE HIGHEST LEVEL ON RECORD

Sentier Research, analyzing data from the Census Bureau's Current Population Survey, reported that the measure of median household income reached $65,666 in December 2019. This is the highest ever recorded for those middle earners, exceeding previous records set in 2017 and 2018.

"Net worth held by the bottom 50 percent of households has increased by 47 percent, more than three times the rate of increase for the top 1 percent of households," the White House Council of Economic Advisers noted. "Real take home pay for the typical middle-class family has increased by roughly $5,000. And, at more than $66,000, real median household income is now at the highest level ever recorded," the Economic Advisers report said, citing economic estimates.

The record-level median household income reached under President Trump flat out defied the fearmongering headlines and absurd predictions pushed by an adversarial press, Trump's political opponents, and a carousel of economists.

Fearmongering in the Media

- "Donald Trump's Economic Plans Would Destroy the U.S. Economy," said *The Atlantic* in May 2016.
- "If Donald Trump is elected, I would expect a protracted recession to begin within 18 months. The damage would be felt far beyond the United States," said former Treasury secretary Larry Summers in June 2016 of an economic calamity that never was.
- "Trump is a one-man crisis for the GOP," read a three-named byline in July 2016 from the ABC News–owned analysis site FiveThirtyEight.
- "The Republican nominee is unfit to serve as president," said President Obama in August 2016 of Donald Trump.
- "We can only hope he won't bankrupt the country," said Nobel Prize–winning economist Joseph Stiglitz in September 2016.
- "A President Trump Could Destroy the World," shrieked an October 2016 *Washington Post* editorial page headline.

U.S. Census Bureau data showed that median household income—that's adjustable gross income or income left after tax—in the United States in 2016 was $59,039. The figure ticked up to $61,372 the following year. By 2018 it had jumped to $63,179.

The Sentier Research data, published by two former Census analysts, is not perfect but is statistically reliable, advanced estimates of economic growth from month to month. Drawing on the Sentier data, former Reagan administration Privatization Commission research director Stephen Moore noted that "real median household income—the amount earned by those in the very middle—hit $65,084 (in 2019 dollars) for the twelve months ending in July. That's the highest level ever and a gain of $4,144, or 6.8 percent, since Mr. Trump took office."

"By comparison, during seven and a half years under President Obama—starting from the end of the recession in June 2009 through January 2017—the median household income rose by only about $1,000," Moore wrote in a September 2019 *Wall Street Journal* op-ed.

50.

AGREEING WITH PRESIDENT TRUMP, 84 PERCENT OF AMERICANS DISTRUST INFORMATION FROM THE CHINESE GOVERNMENT ABOUT THE CORONAVIRUS

The governments of the United States and China became embroiled in a massive worldwide media and political struggle to shape the political narrative around the coronavirus pandemic, beginning almost as soon as the first cases were reported beyond China's borders. China had a lot of advantages in this heavyweight geopolitical slugfest, but six months after the pandemic began, U.S. opinion polls showed President Donald Trump winning the information war.

China's advantages in a battle to control media narratives are obvious. The authoritarian communist nation does not allow dissent from its own people and cuts them off from as much foreign media as possible. Influential social media platforms, including President Trump's personal favorite, Twitter, are banned for average Chinese citizens, but Chinese government officials, state-run media operations, and disinformation campaigns make extensive use of them anyway. Chinese activity on Twitter surged over 100 percent in April 2020, generating almost 100,000 tweets as part of the coronavirus information war.

In addition to this one-sided use of social media to spread its propaganda, China has tremendous influence over American media organizations. The Chinese Communist Party (CCP) does not hesitate to punish foreign newspapers and television networks that displease it, as when reporters for the *Wall Street Journal* were kicked out of Beijing in February 2020 because their newspaper dared to publish an editorial that injured the CCP's pride. Any news organization owned by a company that also creates entertainment media has to worry about its products getting blocked from the lucrative Chinese market.

The CCP doesn't always have to use threats and economic leverage to force American media to convey its narratives, especially at a time when many in the press appear to regard every adversary of President Trump as a potential ally.

For example, with astonishing speed in March 2020, U.S. media outlets almost universally decided that referring to COVID-19 as the "Wuhan virus" or "Chinese virus" was racist, even though many of the same media organizations had been using similar terms themselves, and previous high-profile pandemics have routinely been named after the location of the initial outbreak. Ebola is named after a river in the Congo, for example, while the Zika virus is named after a forest in Uganda. These names aren't always exotic, mind you. Lyme disease, for example, is named for the world's first cluster in Lyme, Connecticut. Trump calling COVID-19 the "Chinese virus" was all it took to make most of the American media establishment instantly adopt the Chinese Communist Party's position that the disease should not be associated with China or the city of Wuhan.

And yet, despite all these advantages, Pew Research Center polls published in April and May 2020 found large majorities of Americans agreeing with President Trump about the importance of banning travel from China to halt the spread of the coronavirus and expressing their deep distrust of the information the communist regime in Beijing was sharing with the world.

In one poll, Pew found unfavorable opinions of China among Americans reaching their highest level since Pew began polling on China in 2005. Sixty-six percent of respondents said they had a negative view of China, a twenty-point increase since President Trump came into office. Another 70 percent said they did not trust Chinese president Xi Jinping. China was given lower ratings for its handling of the pandemic than any other country.

A whopping 84 percent of poll respondents said they distrusted information from the Chinese government about the coronavirus, and 49 percent said they had absolutely no trust in China's statements at all. Just half as many people lacked trust in the World Health Organization (WHO), which has been accused of spreading false information about the pandemic provided by China. Pew found Republicans significantly more likely to distrust and disapprove of the Chinese government than Democrats. But even strong majorities of Democrats expressed a negative view of the regime.

Pew's other poll from the same period found more doubt and suspicion about China from Americans, once again with greater intensity from Republicans. This poll found 59 percent continue to see the United States as the world's leading economic power, versus only 30 percent for China, at a moment when China is aggressively trying to use the coronavirus pandemic to increase its power and influence around the world. Sixty-two percent of respondents agreed that China represents a "major threat" to the United States, while only 48 percent thought so in 2018.

Pew researchers pointed out that public opinion has been shifting against China throughout the Trump presidency. But it didn't grow dramatically worse during the pandemic itself. Negative views of China appear to have hardened in early March. Young people seem to have changed their opinions about China the most since President Trump's election, possibly because they are increasingly aware of China's human rights and environmental abuses and its cyberespionage activities. Older Americans already viewed the communist regime in a very negative light.

The turning of public opinion against China occurred despite a sustained CCP propaganda campaign using everything from social media to stories pushed through the American press. China put a great deal of effort into presenting itself as the champion of globalism during the trade war, constantly contrasting its supposedly internationalist outlook with President Trump's "isolationism." One of the favorite expressions of Chinese diplomats and opinion writers is "win-win cooperation," which implies working with Beijing brings benefits to everyone involved.

China's influence with international organizations grew at a rapid pace over the past few years, thanks in part to the investments made through its Belt and Road Initiative (BRI), originally presented as an attempt to rebuild the Silk Road trade route of antiquity. China took steps to outright subvert international bodies like the World Health Organization, spending copious amounts of money to buy influence to get its favored candidates into top spots.

As globalists grew increasingly frustrated with President Trump's policies, such as pressuring NATO members to meet their financial obligations or withdrawing from the Paris climate accords, China was always there to whisper promises of "win-win cooperation" in their ears. There was a proliferation of op-eds declaring American influence on the wane as China's ascended. Among the globalist set, including influential members of the American press and political establishments, there was no doubt the American Century had ended; all that remained was to quibble over the precise date of its demise.

And yet, as these Pew polls indicate, very few Americans—including very few Democrats—believe China is now the ascendant power, or that China is a trustworthy member of the international community, or that bending to China's demands is in the best interests of America or any other free nation. Despite its immense size and expense, China's propaganda war has been a flop. Those thousands of Twitter accounts created by the communist regime don't appear to be influencing anyone.

Chinese power over Hollywood is a matter of growing concern, not a path to shaping American opinion. People are noticing how criticism of China has vanished over the years from the movies made by a Hollywood entertainment culture that never tires of raging against their own country's alleged sins. Actors who see America as a slave nation, one step away from a white supremacist Nazi take-over, are curiously silent about a Chinese regime that has actual con-centration camps and slave labor. Consumers of those entertainment products are not happy at the idea of censors in Beijing dictating the content of American movie scripts. Movies that overtly seek to glorify China, like Matt Damon's *The Great Wall*, were spectacular flops.

The general public has come a long way toward agreeing with President Trump about China, even as virtually every step he has taken—from the trade war to the coronavirus emergency—has been criticized in the strongest terms by Democrats in politics and the es-tablishment media. The president's critics would be unlikely to give him much credit for persuasiveness, and messaging from the Trump White House is often inconsistent or downright confusing, but there is something to be said for simply being right about issues that are not as nuanced as the media likes to pretend, and using major events to highlight truths that should have been obvious all along. With regard to the threat of communist China, the American people are about as close as ever to reaching a consensus, and it hews far closer to the perspective of Donald Trump than that of his critics.

ACKNOWLEDGMENTS

To my editor, Eric Nelson, without whose guidance and wisdom this book would not be possible. Thank you to my colleagues at Breitbart News and its leadership, Larry Solov, Jon Kahn, and Alexander Marlow, for their endless counsel and support. To Colin Madine, Frances Martel, Sean Moran, John Hayward, and Kristina Wong. Their expertise and assistance in the research herein made this a better book. To my family, for their unending love and encouragement.

ABOUT THE AUTHOR

Jerome Hudson lives in Jacksonville, Florida, with his cat, Oreo.